Sally and Me

By

Constance May Waddell

Artwork by Wendel Norton

ISBN: 0-7596-7994-0

This book is printed on acid free paper.

1stBooks - rev. 3/19/02

Dedication

I dedicate this book:
to all Sally's children and grandchildren,
to all my children and grandchildren, and
to all of Joe's descendents.

Notes from the Author

This is a promise kept. As I discovered childhood diaries in a musty old trunk, I knew the time had come to keep my pledge to my dearest friend Sally, as she lay dying.

I would write down our adventures and the way we experienced that last summer together.

These are the stories and secrets as seen through the eyes of a little girl of twelve in a different time and a different place. Every adventure actually happened. I hope they'll capture for you the fun we had. May you experience how different it was to live in an era when children could safely catch rides with strangers and when it was not unusual for whole families to work together in a business. May you also identify with the universal feelings of being sad and happy at the same time and growing beyond childhood confusion to the beginnings of assurance.

Acknowledgements

… Love for my dear husband, Don, who cooked, cleaned, and encouraged me as he tip-toed 'round my computer during those revolting days of re-writing and kept insisting I had a winner.

…Gratitude for my editor Betsy Brown, who lent her publishing expertise to patiently guide me through editing to finished manuscript.

…Cheers for every member of Northwest Arkansas Writers' Guild who both cheered and corrected me week after week as we labored through the birth of *Sally and Me*.

…Lighted candles for those who caringly critiqued and who shed helpful light on my fledgling novel: Wes and Louise Norton, T. Reid Norton, Carol Linebarger Westby, Gil Fite, Harlene Bass, Alice Ann Knisely, Peggy Twibell, Peggy Parks, Faye Weaver, and Peggy Mann.

…Salutes to Larry Brown who consulted with me about how to promote a novel and to Rebecca Busby who introduced me to novel new ways to make my computer perform.

…Thanks to the Wes Nortons who gifted me with a laptop, to A.D. and T. Reid Norton who gifted me with a video promo from *Norton Brothers Productions*, San Francisco and to A.D. Norton for brochure design.

…Kudos to my fellow creator, Wendel Norton, whose illustrations made this book a work of art.

…And to Wendel's wife/partner, Elizabeth Norton, who kept *Norton Arts* rolling while he drew the illustrations.

Table of Contents

Prologue

1938

"She's coming, She's coming," I sang as I scuffed my feet through the hot sand on the road in front of Grandmother's house. When I'd arrived in Shamrock, Oklahoma three months ago my feet were so tender I'd have to hop from one to the other to keep them from burning. Now they were tough as the soles of my shoes. I sat down on the broken sidewalk and pushed my tanned feet up and back. The hot crystals oozed between my toes and felt warm and comforting.

Today everything felt good. Mother was coming at last. I loved Grandmother with all my heart. She let me help her carry water to her tiny garden every morning and hoe a little bit. When I got tired, she'd let me play with the hollyhock dolls made of flowers that had fallen off during the night. They looked like they had little heads and bodies with skirts of purple, orange, or yellow. We'd carry in a basket of vegetables and she'd always let me put one tomato on the block of ice in the icebox. By the middle of the morning when the sun made her little home unbearable, it was fun to sit out on the steps and scrape my teeth across the ice-cold skin of the tomato. The slushy mixture slid down my throat and I could feel the cold juice all the way down to my tummy.

But at night, I missed my mother's kisses and hugs and Daddy's gruff good night. I even missed my big brother, W. T.'s scary stories. Mother always came and got in bed with me if I had a bad dream, but here in Oklahoma I didn't even mention bad dreams. Once, I had one and Grandmother came and brought me a big dose of Nervine tonic—her cure for everything. So I just kept still and sank further down in the feather mattresses that were piled on my bed because there was no room to store anything else in the one tiny closet.

Grandmother was almost always serious. She was most serious about three things: being good, not borrowing, and praying—lots.

xi

I heard her at night as she knelt by her bed and begged God to reach her daughters and make them Christian. This puzzled me because I was sure that Mother was already a Christian, but I didn't interrupt. I just prayed my own prayers to God that the summer would pass fast so that I could go back to Arkansas and not be homesick any more.

"Well—I'll miss my grandmother and my cousins," I said out loud because it didn't seem right that I was so happy to go. And, of course, I'd miss Grandmother's milk goat, "Deer." I had named her, played with her, fed her, and learned to love her milk. It had tasted funny at first, but later, I wanted it with every meal.

The sun was straight overhead now. My head felt like it had a pulse beat in it. It was like my heart beating up there, I thought. I looked straight up at the sun and then remembered it wasn't good for my eyes. Everything looked blurry.

"Connee, Connee, Connee!" I heard in my stupor. It was my mother calling. It was Mother. There was the car. Mother was here! I grabbed her around the waist and buried my head into that sweet fragrance. Mother wrapped her arms around me. I was home.

On the trip back to Bella Vista where we lived, I couldn't stop chattering. There was so much to tell. "You know there were Terrapin contests every Saturday night on the square? Guess who won second place?" I talked fast and couldn't get enough of looking at her.

"It's a trick, you know. I taught him to come when I whistled. See, they made a big round outline in the sand and set all the turtles in the middle. The one who came out of the circle first was the winner. They had painted numbers on them so they could tell which one belonged to you. Every day at Grandmother's, I took him out of his box and practiced him to come to get his food when I whistled. I just know that's what did it."

Mother smiled and listened to every word I said as if it were the most important in the world. "Did you win something?" she asked, looking straight ahead at the road.

"Oh yes—a big, red pocket knife. It had all kinds of attachments like scissors and a screwdriver and a nail file. But it was a boy gift so I gave it to cousin Lloyd."

"Too bad honey, we could have cut our watermelon with it."

That was just like Mother, she always brought surprises for our trip. She'd made her oatmeal cookies with black walnuts that I loved so much.

We ate them with our sandwiches and bananas. The banana was very special. We didn't have many at Grandmother's or at home since they were so expensive. Mother asked me if I didn't want something else. Then she reached in the sack and pulled out my favorite candy bar—a Snickers. On the square of a little town, we stopped at a drug store and had chocolate ice cream sodas. Back in the car, we talked about how much better we could make sodas at the fountain in Bella Vista.

Late that afternoon, when we crossed the state line, we stopped and stood beside the car to see if we could smell the difference in the Arkansas air. We could. There was a hamburger stand there too. I ate and ate.

I had just asked when school started when Mother told me something that took away my appetite. Well, maybe the surprises had something to do with it too. When Mother told me that it was two and a half more weeks until the summer cottage owners would go home from Bella Vista, I dreaded to hear what came next. I rolled down the window feeling sick. Mother pulled over to the side of the road and I lost all those wonderful treats.

"Yes," Mother tried to be cheery about it as she wiped my face with her wet handkerchief. "You can't stay with us yet because we'll still be working at the resort all day and running the dances at night. It will be all right, though. A wonderful family has invited you to stay with them in their cottage. They have a little girl about your age and her name is Sally. You seemed so homesick when I called that I just had to come to get you. And Honey, I was lonesome to see you, too."

I put on a big smile to make her feel better, but inside I was crying. My tummy felt like it was filled up with a big rock.

Mother drove straight to the Pavilion. It was after dark and the orchestra boys were already tuning up to play for the dance. I opened the door of the car the second it stopped and ran up on the wooden floor toward a figure that I knew so well. Daddy saw me and opened up his arms to swoop me up. I ran into them.

I began to talk fast and gave him the soap animal I'd carved for him in Bible School. He listened for a few minutes, but I knew, like always, that he must get back to work. Mother fixed a cot for me in the back of the restaurant and I went in there to get ready for bed. I smiled so both of my parents would feel free to do their jobs.

It was hard to go to sleep because I loved listening to the music above me in the ballroom. Several times, I sneaked out to get a glimpse of

Mother in her sky blue chiffon evening gown. She looked so beautiful sitting there in the booth at the foot of the stairs. I watched her sparkling smile as she sold each ticket. It was heaven to be where I could see her face. Tomorrow night I'd be in a strange bed—but for now, I was with Mother and Daddy. I pulled the covers over my head and fell asleep. There would be no nightmares tonight.

Chapter 1

Kitty Thirteen
1942

"WAIT, Sally. Wait. He'll hurt you!" I tried to take the crawdad from my friend by getting hold of its body behind its head, but Sally held it high. Laughing and jumping around she sang, "I caught it, I caught it, I fin-al-lee caught it!" Then she let out a loud "yaou!" She tried to fling the crawdad off her hand but it clamped down tight with its pinchers. The harder she flung, the deeper it pinched. "I don't like youoo!" she screamed. Finally, that old crawdad gave up and turned loose. It dropped into the tiny creek below and skittered under a rock.

Sally fell down on the creek bank. She shook and made funny noises. I sat down beside her and put my hand on her back. "Don't cry. I've been pinched so many times. It'll be okay, real soon, I promise. Really!"

I pushed my hands gently under her face and she looked up. "You ninny, don't worry, it's just that—he's so—silly." She put her head down again and sputtered into laughter.

"You're laughing? You're the ninny. I'll make you laugh!" I began tickling Sally who laughed harder and then wriggled away and lay on her tummy watching the creek rush along below her.

I hoped that she would give up the idea of catching more crawdads. Ever since I'd told her that sometimes my brother fried their tails, she'd been eager to try it. She'd even sneaked a little black skillet and some grease from her cottage. It was fun picking up kindling for a small campfire but she didn't know that even if I had caught a million crawdads, I always turned them loose. I couldn't stand the thought of killing them for their tails.

We sat for a while without saying a word. I was thinking of how much I liked Sally. We could be right in the middle of things and stop talking as long as we wanted to. I didn't know anyone else so much like me. We both loved adventures and make believe and switching subjects and reading under the covers.

Of course, there was one way that we were different. Her mother and daddy were rich, I guess. At least, they were able to come every summer for the whole three months and not work. Not like my parents. They ran the Bella Vista Summer Resort for the Linebargers and they worked such long hours that they couldn't even keep me at home.

The Matofskys—that was Sally's last name—always came June 1st at the beginning of "the Season." Mr. Matofsky had to stay at home in Tulsa and work during the week but he came almost every weekend. He was an important realtor. He told Daddy he wanted his family to keep cool so he brought them all to Bella Vista, away from the hot city. Sally, Mrs. M (that's what I called her mother the first time I met them because their name was so hard to say), Joe (Sally's big brother) and their Swedish maid, Hilda, all came. They even brought along their black and white water spaniel, Lady.

Sally asked me a question, and it was just like she'd been thinking thoughts with me. "How many years have we been knowing each other?" she asked.

"This is the fourth summer I've stayed with y'all," I answered.

"Well that first time you were only with us two weeks at the end of the season before the resort closed and you went home," she reminded me.

"Right. And last summer I got to spend nights with you when Mother had to fire that mean baby sitter, and I worked at the fountain at the Pavilion in the daytime, remember?"

"I wish you hadn't had to leave each day."

"But you sure loved the chocolate malts I made you," I teased.

I was quiet again, thinking how glad I was that year when the Matofskys had invited me to stay with them in their cottage instead of spending all three months with Grandmother. I loved her, but I missed the swimming pool and horseback riding and paddling flatboats on the lake and helping serve Cokes at the Pavilion. Most of all, I missed Mother and Daddy. Of course, I still missed them, even while I was staying at the Matofsky's cabin. I began to sink into a familiar sad feeling.

Sally reached over and squeezed my hand. "Want to go wading?" Without waiting for an answer, she kicked off her shoes and stuck her feet in the icy spring water. My sad mood was gone. I could never feel lonely for long with Sally around because she always had something going. Life

2

was really fun with her. I peeled off my shoes and socks too and began wading with her on the slippery rocks.

"Shhh! SSSHH!" Sally had her finger on her lips and her head turned to hear better. "Did you hear that?"

I listened. The water from Big Spring gushed out from under an overhang forming the little creek that splashed over rocks, making a melody like wind chimes tinkling in the wind. I stood looking at our feet, numb and blue with cold, and strained to hear. Then came a pitiful noise. It sounded like a raspy whistle.

Two attempts to cough and a "rrreow"—and then a stronger "RREOW," very near us.

It was caught in the bushes on the edge of the bank. I darted my hand in and latched onto a little critter covered with mangy hair. Cuddling it close, I felt its tiny claws sink into my arms. The thin little body shook with fear, but its fiery blue eyes flashed as it let out a ferocious hiss.

"Ooo, it's a kitty." Sally cooed in sweet tones. She reached to take it from my arms.

"Wait, Sally. Remember the crawdad? This one's a biter!"

She waited. I held the kitten close, stroking its awful hair and petting its skinny little back. Both of us sat on an old log and talked to it in motherly tones. It began to relax and I could feel it working up to purring. Its noises were a little hoarse but it started kneading its paws against me and I knew it was feeling safe.

Sally jumped up. "Okay. She's settled down. I think Mom will let us keep it, but first we have to get it clean. She hates things not clean."

Before I could get up, she grabbed the kitty from my arms and said in a big voice as if she were announcing it before a crowd, "I know what we'll do. We'll give this kit-cat a bath in this nice clean water."

"Oh, I don't think she'll like that!"

I screamed for her to wait, but she headed for the creek. Before I could catch her, Sally dunked that tiny kitty under the ice-cold water. This time the "YEEOW" was a thousand times louder than before.

"She didn't like it," Sally said in a mournful voice.

Before I could agree, the cat let out another strong "rreau" that reminded me of a baby's helpless cry, and then stiffened in Sally's hands.

"Oh no. I'm a bat brain! I killed it, Connee, I killed it!"

She began to run, clutching the stick-like body. I whisked up the black skillet and the rest of our things and ran after her.

3

"Where are you goin'? Where are you GO-in?" I called out, trying to catch up with her.

"To the cottage. I'm going to the cottage. I'm going to see my MOM!" she yelled without looking back.

I streaked down the narrow dirt road and passed the corner where our house was. I wished Mother were there. Boy, I wouldn't have taken that kitten to Mrs. M. Sometimes she scared me she was so stern. Just the opposite of Mother—Mother was so warm and friendly, but Mrs. M seemed sort of mad lots of the time. You could be pretty sure she wouldn't like how we made our beds or cleaned the bathtub. Her voice would sound like she was tired of trying to get us to "do it the right way." What was Sally thinking of, taking a dead kitty to Mrs. M?

Sally began trying to whistle their whistle as she got on the path to their cottage. All the Matofskys used this family whistle. She couldn't make her lips work. She slowed down and I ran up beside her and looked at the cat. Its lips were stretched open but its teeth were clamped tight. I felt sick. Sally began to yell for her mother. I began to yell for her too.

Mrs. M must have heard us. She was standing with the screen door open. She took one look at Sally's mournful face and then reached out and took the stiff kitten. She picked up a towel that Sally's brother Joe, had thrown across a chair, and then carefully wrapped the rigid form in it. "MOM!" Sally began to wail again. Mrs. M actually smiled a little—more to herself than to us. She carried the bundle into the bathroom and laid it on the floor in front of the gas heater. Sally and I followed her in and knelt down by it.

Joe and the maid, Hilda, stood watching from the doorway. "Well, you've done it now, haven't you Scrawny?" Joe taunted me.

Sally always tried to protect me. She snapped at him. "She didn't do anything. I did it. Just shut up, Joe."

"Hush," Mrs. M scolded. It was the first word she'd said since we'd come in with the corpse. "Joe," she said calmly, "go and bring me a couple of kitchen matches."

She then lit the bathroom gas stove and unwrapped the towel a little to expose the kitty's body to the heat. It looked so skinny with its wet hair plastered to its sides. I shuddered. It made me think of a dead rat Mother had carried up one time out of the cellar.

"Well, I'll go dig a grave, you little killers."

"Oh, no! I'm a bat brain. I killed it, Connee, I killed it!"

"Joe, I told you that I'm the one who did it!" There were tears in Sally's voice. He didn't say any more.

I could hear the clock ticking. No one spoke. It seemed forever that we all watched and waited like statues. I wondered what we were waiting for. More time passed, then I saw Sally's mother begin to smile. She leaned down to the bundle. A raspy purr was coming from it as Mrs. M completely unfolded the towel. The kitten was alive! Its teeth weren't together any more and its stiff little body was all relaxed. It even looked like a real kitten with its fur all dry and a bit fluffy.

"What happened?" we all wanted to know at once. Mrs. M explained that she had seen cats in shock before. "Sometimes the warmth brings them out of it," she told us. "Not always, but sometimes. Cats are very resilient."

Sally interrupted her with a hug. I almost felt like hugging her too. But I didn't. I knew though that I'd never be afraid of her again. Mrs. M was okay.

Sally talked her mother into letting her keep the kitty as a new pet. She answered all her objections and promised she would always feed it and brush it and keep it away from Lady, and my dog, Jiggs, who was spending the summer at the Matofsky's cabin. Even when Mrs. M spotted fleas crawling over the kitty's tummy, she convinced her mom that she'd put flea powder on her every single morning.

That night, after Mrs. M had put the kitty in a towel lined box in the bathroom, Sally brought her and cuddled her in bed with us under the covers. She whispered that her mother was asleep. "You know she really expects me to do this," she said. "Mom's really not such a bad person." I didn't answer. Instead, I thought and thought about this new side of Mrs. M.

There were some thoughts and feelings I could only write in my diary or tell God. These had to do with stuff that I was afraid might hurt Sally's feelings. Like my fears of Mrs. M—after all, she was Sally's mother. Then there was my homesickness for Mother and Daddy. I just knew Sally wouldn't understand how I could be lonely when I was with her.

Again, just like she'd read my mind, Sally said, "I'm always at home when I'm with you. You're like a sister." We hugged with the kitty squeezed between us. She meowed.

"Oh, poor thing," I said and petted her, and then she settled down again.

"What are we going to name her?" I asked. "I always, always think everything must have a name. I name our hens in the winter. Remember I told you about my chicken who was blind in her left eye? Ol' One Eye came when I called her name. And, of course, I named my kitties and I even named that mama skunk that had babies under our house. She was Lila. O course, I can't name all the flies that I catch in the vacuum cleaner and take outside to let loose…."

"Oh Connee, STOP! Yes! You're right. We have to name her. I'm thinking. Okay, I got it," Sally announced snapping her fingers. "Kitty Thirteen. This kit-cat has been so unlucky. And I'm thirteen and you'll be thirteen this fall. Let's name her Kitty Thirteen."

"I like it." I smiled in the dark. "Kitty Thirteen. I just hope she'll be lucky with us."

"She already is, 'Scrawny.' She already is."

"Don't call me 'Scrawny.'" I punched her pillow as I said the word. "It's bad enough when Joe does."

"You're right." She hugged me again, this time lifting Kitty Thirteen up to protect her.

"Girls," Mrs. M called. "Mr. Matofsky is trying to sleep." Both of us slammed our heads down on our pillows.

"Friends?" whispered Sally.

"Friends," I whispered back. Kitty Thirteen snuggled between us, purring like a motor.

Chapter 2

Next Day

The next morning I woke up to the sound of Sally and her mother talking. "But—Mom, Connee knows all about training cats. She has dozens of them in the winter. When the people go home, some of them just leave theirs in their cottage and then they find their way to Connee's house. Her mother lets her keep them and in the spring they have babies. She told me people come to her house and pick one up and...."

"Sally, those are outdoor cats. I'm talking about an indoor cat!" Mrs. M seemed exasperated.

Sally was not to be outdone. "Well—she has one of those, too. It's named 'Winery' because Connee's Daddy found it over where they make wine. You know, the Winery right behind the Linebargers' Log House where they make the wine and then they put it in Wonderland Cave to let it get old?" I could hear her mother sigh a loud sigh and Sally stopped talking.

"All right, just make sure that there are no messes in this cottage. You can keep her only if you and Connee can teach her to go outside. Now, you girls go in there and let Hilda give you your breakfast. Connee's up and we need to get this place clean."

I scurried into the bathroom. How did she know that I was up? I felt a little of the old fear of her that I'd had before. In a minute though, Sally came in and I was dressed. "Come look," she smiled, putting her fingers to her lips. She pulled me by the arm into the screened porch and pointed to the little stoop outside at the top of the stairs.

Sally's father was standing there, like he did every weekend morning when he was able to be in Bella Vista. He always came out in his undershirt and gazed down at the haze floating over the lake. Everything looked tiny from up here on the hill. The inlets Sally and I explored were just spidery fingers at one end of a large oval of blue-green water. Even the two-story Pavilion at one end of the lake seemed small enough to pick up and move around like a building in our Monopoly game. It was too early for any of the boats to be rented out yet. Only the birds sailed around in the air, looking down for fish for breakfast.

As usual, Lady and my dog, Jiggs, sat patiently waiting for a signal that it was time for a walk. They both looked out at the lake in the same direction as Sally's dad, as if they were thinking what he was thinking.

I liked seeing Mr. Matofsky. He was a cute little man with a fat tummy and his waist tucked into his shorts. For his walk he wore only his sleeveless undershirt. His stiff brimmed straw hat and the big cigar in the corner of his mouth made me think of a character in the Sunday funnies. But Mother told me that the people on Tulsa Row, the cottages on the road closest to the lake, said that he was a "real sharp businessman." And he was so sweet. When he brought a gift to Sally, there was always one just like it for me. He talked in a kind voice and never called us down—not even Joe. He seemed to leave all that to Mrs. M.

It was always the same scene: big, longhaired Lady and my little shorthaired fox terrier, Jiggs, standing on either side of him waiting at attention. Today though, one thing was added. Sally pointed and smiled. There—rubbing up against Lady's soft fur and purring as loud as her tiny throat could manage, was Kitty Thirteen.

After breakfast and bed making we were ready for what Sally called our "Bella Vista Adventures." We never knew just what they would be, but we were sure there would be some.

"Let's walk over to the Information Booth," I said. "But first, let's stop and see Mother at the Pavilion."

We started out skipping down the dirt trail from the cottage. That wasn't easy. When we got to the place where a steep sidewalk took off down the hill by the Band Stand, a round platform with a roof where the orchestra boys played some Sunday afternoons, we let ourselves go and ran down with our arms outstretched like airplanes.

I let Sally run ahead of me since I'd done it a million times. In winter, when it was freezing cold, my brother, W. T., and I would carry buckets of water over from the swimming pool. As soon as we had poured the first bucketful down the sidewalk from the top of the hill, the ice began to form. We'd go back and forth carrying water for what seemed like hours. Finally there would be our own perfect place to ride our sled on a sheet of ice. W. T. was five years older than I was and a bit bossy. I didn't care

9

though; it was always so great when he would play with me. It was lonely in the winter when all the resort people were gone. And besides, I felt important when he paid attention to me.

When we got to the Pavilion, it was still early enough that there weren't many customers. Mother gave us some fresh squeezed orange juice and a tiny ham sandwich apiece. My favorites! She poured herself a cup of coffee and sat with us in one of the metal ice cream parlor chairs around the small round table. I loved this place with its big wooden floor. There were no walls, so the soft wind from the lake blew through like a gentle fan. Later, the tables would be filled with people eating hamburgers and drinking Coca Colas. It was cool upstairs in the ballroom and sometimes women played bridge there in the afternoons.

"Honey, I have some news for you. And I don't know how you are going to take it." She rushed on before I could say anything. "You know that W. T. had planned to work at the resort all summer. Daddy and I wanted you to have this last summer before you became a teenager just playing with Sally. But W. T. has this chance to begin work at Hemphill Book Store near the campus of the University of Texas where he starts college this fall. He'd make a lot more money there than he could here, waiting tables at the dance for tips. The book store will pay him a real salary and there's no one else to get to work here at this last minute…"

"And you want me to go to work?" I finished for her. She nodded and reached over to pat my hand as if she wanted to say how sorry she was. I had to be careful not to say anything to hurt Sally's feelings. How could I explain to my dearest friend in the whole world that the idea of going back to work thrilled me? It wasn't that I didn't love to be with the Matofskys, but to run the swimming pool all day and, for the first time, to wait tables at the dance at night and to be near Mother and Daddy? That sounded too good to be true.

Mother saved me by saying, "Look at the bright side. He doesn't leave until the first of July so that gives you all the rest of June to play together." Some boys came up to buy candy so Mother got busy.

"That's sure not like having the whole summer." Sally mumbled to herself under her breath. We waved at Mother and took off for the Spillway—a wide, low place where the lake ran over the road and made a pretty waterfall as it fell down over huge flat rocks into Sugar Creek on the other side. It had cement blocks for stepping-stones and looked a lot more inviting today than in the winter when it was cold. Sometimes when

10

I walked over to the highway to catch the bus for school, my shoes got wet from the spray and then I had to sit in class all morning with cold feet.

Sally was still quiet when we got to the other side. "This year I've walked to the bus alone every morning," I said, trying to get us talking again. "It's at least a half-mile from home, across the Spillway and two bridges to the highway. W. T. rode his bike all the way to town so that he could stay and practice football after school."

"Mikedosh! You mean he rode five miles each way? What about that big Braithwaite Hill?"

"He had to walk his bike up part of it but mostly he rode," I said, my voice sounding strong with pride. I liked Sally saying "mikedosh," too. It was something I'd told her we said at school. The teachers called us down when we said "my gosh." So at recess we started saying "m'gosh" and later it turned into "mikedosh."

"I just don't see why W. T. can't work here this summer," she muttered under her breath again.

"Well—see—Uncle C. A. Linebarger, the owner of Bella Vista, only pays one salary. That's to my daddy." I took her hand and we stepped on each block together. "This spring, W. T. tried to make some money picking potatoes up in Maine, but it rained the whole time. He tried to join the army too, but he's what you call '4F'—something about his blood pressure. He tried twice but they turned him down. I feel so sorry for him but I think Mother is happy he can't enlist. She says it's wonderful that he is going to try college. I don't mind, Sally. I'll save part of my tips and I can buy sweaters for school and—I like to work. I'll really—truly—miss getting to be with you all the time, though." I'd told the truth and that felt good. Strangely, as soon as I did, the loss of being with Sally became real to me.

We leaned out over the bridge rail looking into the lake for a long time. My explanation must have helped her because suddenly, she whirled around and looked me right in the eyes.

"Bonnie Connee, I have the most scrumptious idea! Let's choose a different adventure for each day. There are twenty-five days left. We'll take turns thinking them up on our own and surprise each other."

"And you have to do what the other one says, no matter what it is— even if you don't want to," I entered in wholeheartedly. "I like it. We can start right now. Today. And you can choose first."

11

"I've got it already," she said and began skipping to the second bridge. "Let's go to the Information Booth and decorate it with colored water." It had fascinated Sally when I told her that every year before the resort opened, we squeezed colored crepe paper into water and filled empty pop bottles with red, blue or yellow.

I had planned to do the job with Alice Hobbs, one of the few other kids who lived in Bella Vista all year round. But we couldn't because she'd been sick. Should I wait until she could help or go on with it and do what Sally wanted? It was a hard decision and I was relieved when Uncle Elmer said he really didn't want to wait any longer to get them up.

The ledge above the Information Booth sign would hold exactly twenty bottles. Uncle Elmer, my daddy's brother, ran the place on the highway. People who were driving through or who were renting cottages for a couple of weeks and wanted to know more about Bella Vista, stopped for a cold drink and asked him questions.

In the back storeroom were the buckets and stacks of crepe paper. First, we had to wash the pop bottles until they were sparkling clean. Then we swished a different color of paper in each bucket of water. Sally showed me how to mix colors together, to make green or brown or fuchsia. They taught her in art classes in her school in Tulsa. I couldn't believe they had an art teacher and a music teacher. We didn't have either one. In Bentonville our music lesson was to go to Assembly and sing "Old McDonald" or "Cowboy Jack."

When we had all the colors made, we poured them in the bottles and took them around front for Uncle Elmer to cap. He bragged on us, and he even let us climb the ladder to put them on top of the building. The three of us stood back and admired how beautiful the bright colors looked with the sun shining through the glass.

"Well, bye, Uncle Elmer," Sally said and started walking away. "What's next?" she sort of sang out.

"It's still your choice." I sang back.

"It has to be Sunset Trail! What else?" she said, trotting off down the highway. It was only about a fourth of a mile to the curving path that led us up to the top to the Sunset Hotel. I held back. I was so used to climbing up and down these Ozark hills that it didn't make me tired at all, but Sunset Trail was steep. Sally was a city girl nine months of the year and the summer was just starting. I thought she'd need to stop at each landing

12

and sit on the bench to rest. She surprised me though. Instead, we both kept climbing and panting and made it to all the way to the crest.

There we were in front of the huge white three-story building that looked out over the whole resort. You could see it as far as five miles away, like a beacon watching over everyone. White rocking chairs with tall backs and wide armrests lined the second floor porch. We climbed the stairs and each plopped down in one and began to rock. "Hey, you can see the saddle barn and the swimming pool and the Pavilion and—oh, look, I see our cottage!" Sally said. "This is the best!"

"Ummm," I agreed. "Have I told you about Daddy saving the hotel?" Sally stopped rocking and looked interested. So I started into my story. I could talk to Sally better than anyone in the world. She always made me feel that what I was saying was important and intelligent. She understood and she never told anyone else. Not that this was a secret, and maybe it would seem like bragging, but somehow I knew she'd love to hear it as much as I'd love to tell it.

"He was sick in bed, you know—with the flu. Mother said she was glad it was winter because that way he could be indoors and get good and well. She'd gone to Bentonville for groceries and I was staying with him in case he needed anything. She was worried about leaving him, but Daddy had a real high fever and we were out of aspirin. All morning he'd fretted about all the jobs he needed to do. Mother told him he always worked harder than any of his crew getting the cottages and the roads repaired and that he'd just have to get well first.

I was deep into reading. You know how I love to read. It was the fifth time I'd read this Oz book—not the *Wizard of Oz* but one of the others. I thought he was asleep. Then, all of a sudden, here came my daddy running through the room with nothing on but his pajamas! He ran out the door, jumped in his coupe and drove off so fast that his tires spun a lot of gravel into the air."

"Why? Why'd he do that?" Sally interrupted. She leaned forward in the rocker. I could see excitement in her eyes and I got excited, too.

13

"He single handedly SAVED THE SUNSET HOTEL!"

"It was the Sunset Hotel. He had been lying there in bed looking up at it across the valley and thinking about how long it had taken him and the men to build it. They'd aged the wood a whole year and he said that it would last a long, long time. Anyway, he had been lying there half asleep when something he saw jerked him awake. There was smoke coming out of the hotel roof! He jumped up and ran to the window. It was true. The Sunset was on fire! And do you know what he did? He blew his car horn all the way up the mountain. He beat everyone else there, so he grabbed a tow sack out of his rumble seat and rushed over to a faucet and got it real wet. By the time others came, he had climbed up a ladder and beat out the fire with that wet sack. He single handedly SAVED THE SUNSET HOTEL!"

I was standing up by now and I shouted the words out over the banister. I'll bet I yelled loud enough for everyone to hear all the way over to the Matofsky's cottage.

Sally was thrilled, I could tell. We sat there smiling. "Your daddy is a hero, no doubt about it. I've always looked up to him. There's just one thing I don't know, though. What in the world is a tow sack?"

I laughed. "It's real rough material. Scratchy. Our cow feed and lots of stuff you buy comes in them. Daddy said it's made out of burlap or jute like his binder twine. He carries a bunch of them in the car all the time and he has his crew keep them in their trucks. If a fire breaks out on these hills the cottages will burn and we're too far out of town for a fire truck to come save us. Everyone who lives in Bella Vista knows how to beat out fires, and Bentonville, too. Once, on Sunday, there was a big, big fire over on Louisiana Mountain. They rang the church bells and carloads of people came out here and helped put it out."

"Oh," Sally said. "Horse feathers! I wish I could be here to put out a fire some time."

"I wish you lived here all year round," I said, meaning it with all my heart. "Well, let's go in and take a look at the lobby."

Everything was dark and cool when we went in. The ceilings were high and the floor shone like a mirror. There were large golden urns of flowers that sat on the floor.

"This is where they announce people when they go into the dining room," I explained. "They call out their names and there are waiters standing around wearing white coats and white gloves and they have white towels over their arms."

15

"…the huge white three story building…was like a beacon watching over everyone."

"I know," Sally said.

Immediately I remembered her telling me about them coming here. Her mother wore a long evening gown and her daddy and Joe wore suits, and oh my goodness, I wished I hadn't talked so much.

"How do you like those tall green *jardinières*?" Sally said, pointing to the jars of water on each white tablecloth in the dining room.

"Stunning," I answered, using one of her words. I filed away *jardinières* in my mind for future use.

All of a sudden, the headwaiter followed by other waiters and some bell boys, rushed out of the dining room. He was shouting and sounded mad. Sally grabbed my hand and we followed them out into the yard and around to the kitchen entrance. All of them stopped and began pointing. A few laughed but others looked scared. "What are those? Oh, Connee!" Sally squeezed my hand hard. "What are those?"

It was obvious and it was awful. The sight horrified me. Big frogs that had had their legs cut off to be cooked that evening were flopping around all over the grassy hillside. No legs! I hid my eyes. One of the waiters said, "Oh Lordy, Lordy!"

Sally and I turned and started running back down Sunset Trail. Once she tripped and almost fell. We hurried so fast that I slid down and finished the last part of it on my rear end. We laughed a little then looked back up at the hotel and started running again. We passed Uncle Elmer who was talking to some tourists. He looked up just as we scurried past and yelled "Anything wrong?" We just shook our heads and didn't slow down until we got to the bridges. We weren't even careful when we went across the Spillway and we didn't stop until we got back to the cottage.

My sides hurt but all either of us could think of was getting into the bedroom and closing the door. We kept saying, "We're safe, we're safe," and hugging each other. My legs were weak and trembling and Sally's eyes were big. I began to remember those frogs flopping around and both of us kept saying how scared we were. How could they hop with their legs all cut off? It was horrible. Spooky.

"Did you ever feel so scared?" Sally asked.

Immediately a memory came to me. "Yes, one time I was at Grandmother's and I saw a cross in the sky. I was so afraid. I thought it was the end of the world. I just couldn't move. Grandmother found me staring at it and finally got me to tell her what was the matter. I thought she'd be scared, too. Instead, she showed me how the screened door was made up of little cross lines and that what I was seeing was really just the light shining through them on the clouds. She gave me a dose of her Nervine tonic and I felt so dumb."

I'm glad I remembered that story because it made Sally decide to tell her Mother about what we had seen at the hotel. Mrs. M explained to us what she thought had happened.

"They weren't really alive, girls. I think it was just their muscles still flexing around."

Whew. I was relieved and now I felt so tired. We didn't know that Joe had been standing right outside the room while we were talking. He waited until he had our attention and began taunting us by imitating the poor frogs. He jumped around—flopped down on the floor and opened his mouth and rolled his eyes like a crazy man.

Joe you make me so upset, I thought, *Stop it, stop it, please!* Sally called him stupid. Then we all started laughing and it felt better to be laughing at stupid Joe than thinking about those poor frogs. The day hadn't failed us. We'd had our adventure. And now we had our sleep. I didn't even dream bad dreams that night. I just slept. Very hard.

Chapter 3

The Plunge

Dear Diary,

It's early morning and our new Kitty Thirteen is sitting on my lap. I'm out on the screened porch and not a soul is up but me. The lake looks so different, like its dancing with sun diamonds. It's not lonely like at night. I see the two white herons they named Gladys and Whitey for Mother and Daddy in the Bella Vista Breezes newspaper. They said Mother looked like "Jean Harlow," the silvery blonde movie star—my hair is blonde but not light and gorgeous like hers. I'm trying to think what I'll choose for our adventure today. I'm getting hungry for breakfast but I sure dread meals around here. I wish I wouldn't get so nervous!!!!

Love, Connee

Everything was always good until Joe got to the table. I'd unfold my napkin in my lap and plan to eat without a single boo-boo. That morning he was late, as usual. He swung one long leg over the chair and grinned at me, but I ignored him. Joe might have been good looking if he weren't so mean. He had Sally's yummy light cocoa skin and the same wavy golden brown hair. But when I looked at him I had the opposite feeling to when I looked at Sally. Ugh!

Here's what he did to me: He watched me. He even talked about me as if I weren't there. He said, "Well, has Scrawny spilled anything yet? Watch her folks—she's picking up her juice. She's tipping it to her mouth. Look out! There she goes—right on Hilda's white tablecloth. Oops—slop—bring the mop. She's done it again!" Every time, I swore I wouldn't spill. Every time it happened anyway. I wished that he would leave and never, never come back.

Sally said something before her mother could. "Joe, sometimes I wish you would stop being my brother." He took hold of her arm and started to twist it, and Mrs. M made them both leave the table for five minutes. I sat there and wished I could leave, too. When they came back, Sally asked if we could be excused.

"What did you choose?" she asked, shutting our bedroom door.

I was still so sick with embarrassment that I was shaking inside and, at first, I didn't get what she meant. "Oh, well, how about swimming?" I said in a quivery voice.

"Perfect." Sally hugged me. "Let's grab our suits and dress down there."

"After we take Kitty Thirteen outside," I said, making my voice cheerful like hers.

A crowd of kids stood under the big sign that said THE PLUNGE, waiting to buy admissions; so my brother, W. T. waved us on through. He was supposed to be good looking. He had won 2nd place in a bathing beauty contest for swimmers when he was just a little boy. Sally said we looked like identical twins. That was crazy because he was five years older than I was, but we did both have blue eyes and curly blonde hair. Mother and Daddy did too. But of course, Sal knew that a boy and a girl couldn't be identical. She was just teasing.

"Let's go on in," I whispered as we bypassed other kids. "He has real customers."

"And what are we?" She laughed, shaking out her beach towel on the grass by the pool.

"Well, you have a season ticket and I'm just part of the help." We laid out our towels and took turns rubbing suntan lotion on each other. It smelled like coconut—my favorite.

"Connee May. All of us would give our eyeteeth to be you. You get to make milk shakes and sell candy at the Pavilion. You can use the boats and ride horses free and you get to live here all year and your daddy is Mr. May and..."

She shook her thick wavy hair back, wrapped a white towel around it and flopped down on her tummy. I heard her laughing some more and that made me laugh too. I hadn't thought of it like she did. Daddy was always telling me how lucky I was. "Turn off the lights behind you, Connee," I can hear him saying. "Just because we have free lights and water, we don't have to waste them." It was all kind of confusing to be so different from the other girls at the resort. With my friends at school, I thought of us as all being alike.

The sun got hotter and hotter. My back began to beat as if the heat were pounding against it with a rolling pin. I turned to check Sally's back. No, it wasn't burning. Her skin looked like Mother's coffee with lots of cream in it.

Sally was so beautiful. If she were at Bella Vista in the winter, I just knew that Lillian Green would take pictures of her. Lillian was Uncle C. A. Linebarger's secretary. She did photography while he and his wife, Aunt Ray spent their winters in Key West, Florida. I liked it that she sold some pictures of me for magazine covers. Sally was so glamorous. If she lived here, there'd be no question about it. Lillian would put her on all kinds of magazine covers and brochures. She'd be a movie star if a Hollywood talent scout ever saw her. I was so proud to be her best friend.

"Follow the leeeeder," she yelled. She jumped up dropping her towel and ran across the grass to the sidewalk. Grabbing her legs under her knees, she made a big cannonball splash into the pool. Boy, did that wake me up. I was right behind her and for at least a half-hour we took turns. I'd walk back to the fence and walk stiff-legged to the side of the pool and just keep walking until I fell in. She'd do the same. She'd walk in backward or close her eyes and turn 'round and 'round until she was dizzy then open them to lean over and fall into the water. I'd run fast, stick my legs out in front of me and then hit flat in what was called a "preacher's seat".

But the one we liked the very best was to hold your nose, stand with your toes curled over the side of the pool and then lean far out to fall in. If we kept our heads down, our bodies did complete summersaults under the water. It was great.

We were still playing when some of my girlfriends from school came. Sally knew all of them—Jodee and Loudee Boren (the sisters), Janet Wyman, Susie Bolin and Betty Ivy. They joined right in the game, so we just kept giggling and changing leaders. It was fun to have them here together with Sally.

We all trouped over to the Pavilion for cherry Cokes. Mother was there, getting the waitresses ready to serve lunch and I got a hug from her. She felt so soft and warm. Then Susie said, "There go the boys." That tore me away. I squinted my eyes to see if Freddy Allred was with them.

21

They were headed for the pool gate so we grabbed our Cokes and meandered back down the hot sidewalk talking to each other and acting like we didn't see them. Inside, we parked our paper cups on our towels and followed them. Dale Rife looked back at us and said "Well, look who's here." We smiled and pretended we were so surprised to see them. Everyone headed for the Wheel.

Daddy had figured out how to make the white wooden wheel and everyone loved it. It was between the shallow and deep end—deep enough not to hurt yourself. It had steps at the back and you climbed up them, sat down on the wheel and as it turned, it rolled you right off and dropped you into the cool water. The girls squealed and held on to the sides but some of the guys lifted their hands straight up to show how brave they were.

As soon as I plunged in, I swam to the ladder, climbed out and got back in line. Freddy Allred got behind me every time. I had on my one-piece coral bathing suit and wished it were blue instead. Once a friend told me (that a friend had told her) that Freddy said my eyes were so blue when I wore my sky blue dress. I pushed my bathing cap back so that my eyes would show more and looked around at him. He gave me a little push and laughed as I slid down further on the wheel. He lay back with his arms crossed and looked up at the sky like he didn't have a care in the world, then glided down feet first into the water. Finally we got tired and swam together and ended up out at "the Top."

"The Top" was in seven feet of water and you had to be a good swimmer and brave to get on it. It was exactly like the toy tops that go spinning off a string. But this one was at least eight feet wide and had a pipe attached through it to a swivel at the bottom of the pool. If three or four held the steering wheel attached to the pipe, they could run 'round and 'round and it would spin faster and faster until everyone seated around the edge was slung off into the water.

Lots of the kids were already there holding it as level as they could so that others could get on. We spaced ourselves around the edge so it wouldn't tilt. That's the one thing you had to keep it from doing. Once it tipped over on its side, everyone slid off. Those clinging to the top edge slid the farthest. Everyone squealed and yelled and screamed and it was a peck of fun. To climb up the slippery flat side that sticks straight up in the air was hard. Sometimes it took as long as an hour to get it all balanced and ready to spin again.

"...you had to be a good swimmer and brave to get on it."

I sat by Freddie. So did Betty Ivy. Sally told me later that she saw it, too. Instead of paying attention to me, like he always did, he grabbed Betty when she started to slide and she laughed and flirted with him. It made me heart sick. It was like that the rest of the afternoon. Wherever her red head was—there was Freddie's—bent down to hear what cute thing she was saying.

We all sat on our dried out towels—the boys too, and sipped our watery Cokes. Dale talked to me but I wanted to go home. Sally told them about how she'd drawn a picture of the Square at Bentonville for her friends back in Tulsa. As she described the red, white and blue flowers and the statue in the middle and how we all played there on Saturday nights, I could tell that my friends liked how she saw our little town. Ordinarily it would have made me proud. Today, I was miserable.

Back at the cottage, a shower and dry clothes made us feel cozy and hungry after swimming so long. Hilda brought in a plate of warm cookies and milk and stood and waited for Sally and me to say "Ummmmm" like we always did. Sally read and I wrote in my diary, then we took a little nap and it was time to eat supper.

Joe was "in great form," as Mrs. M liked to call it. He was super polite and asked if "Scrawny" could please pass the green peas. I decided not to pay the name calling any attention. Then he turned to Sally and asked her to please pass the potatoes and gravy to "Corny" so that she wouldn't have to do it and spill. Sally started to fuss at him and Mrs. M gave him a dark look but Joe went on. "Now, CccccConnee, your milk glass is very full. Watch her everybody, she's not going to spill. She is NOT going to spill. She is not...." and it sounded like he was announcing a Tiger football game at my school.

I was determined not to spill. Slowly and carefully I picked up my glass and took a dainty sip, then set it down again and smirked at Joe. "Oh, she's good at drinking milk tonight folks," he bantered. "But—her heart is broken and sad now and she'll NEVER LOVE AGAIN."

"What?" I screamed—jumping up and tipping over my milk. Mrs. M stood up and even Mr. Matofsky looked shocked. I'm sure it surprised Sally, too.

I ran out onto the porch. My diary was open to the pages I'd written that afternoon. "F" doesn't like me any more. He likes Betty. M.H.I.B.A.S.N.—I.N.L.A. And then like a dummy, I'd written the meaning of the letters in little bitty words at the bottom of the page. *My Heart Is Broken and Sad Now—I'll Never Love Again.*

I was ruined. Joe had read my diary. I was so ashamed. I ran into the bedroom and fell across the bed.

Mrs. M's voice came through the door. "Go see about her Sally, and Joe, I don't know what this is all about, but you know we have to talk about this right this minute."

I had the pillow over my head and Kitty Thirteen was trying to get to my face. Sally put her head down by mine "I know, I know," she said trying to soothe me. "He makes me so mad. When we are back in Tulsa, sometimes he's real sarcastic to me."

"But why doesn't your mother stop him?" I asked, my voice muffled under the pillow.

"Haven't you noticed? He's her favorite."

I'd never heard Sally so serious and sort of sad sounding. I threw off the pillow and looked at her. She was staring away from me toward the window. I put my hand on her arm and she turned back and we just sat there looking into each other's eyes.

Suddenly a smile came over her face. "Never fear, Connee dear," she spoke in a low mysterious voice. "I know something to get even with my mean brother. He'll be sorry. Listen—you're going to love it."

Chapter 4

Pear Honey

Sally woke me by putting Kitty Thirteen on my face. I felt her soft kneading paws and little nibbles on my cheek. Gently, I pulled her away and held her to me petting her and running my finger under her chin. Her hair was growing out and beginning to get fluffy. She was definitely a little Calico with yellows and browns and whites splashed with orange and gray. I was pretty sure Calicos are always girls.

"Ready?" Sally whispered. Her dark brown eyes sparkled with mischief and I remembered what she'd said the night before about getting even with Joe.

"Let me snooze just a few more minutes." I was groggy and kind of reluctant to hear the plan for the day. Sally snuggled back down in the covers and began stroking Kitty's fur, too. The dark olive skin on her arm looked so rich beside my white one. No matter how tan I got, I couldn't match her pretty complexion. Her face shone in the sunlight coming through the windows.

In a minute, I sighed, "Okay, I'm ready. But what about your mother and Joe?"

"That's just it, my beautiful one! They left for a fishing trip before daylight. With Dad and Hilda back in the city, we've got the whole place to ourselves—including JOE'S ROOM." And with that, she began stalking out of the bedroom—taking long steps. She grabbed a coat from a hook and then slinked through the door staying close to the wall. I recognized her imitation of Dick Tracy, the detective in the funny papers.

I followed her—just walking—so she gave up her act and started toward the outside stairs where Jiggs and Lady sat waiting and watching in case someone would come take them for a walk.

My tummy told me it was time for breakfast but I followed her. As we went down the stairs, I began to be excited that, at last, I was going into that forbidden territory where Joe disappeared each night.

We raced down the last few steps, "This looks like where the dirty scoundrel lives." Sally had returned to the deep voice of the detective.

Inside, the room was long and dark. It was the length of the whole cabin but narrower. The carport connected to his windows and cut off lots of light. Still, there were the trees to enjoy and a clear view of the lake below. It was cool and restful and I liked it.

Sally pulled the chain on the bulb that hung down from the ceiling and I began to look at all his stuff. Exciting. One table held a whole collection of arrowheads. He'd marked each one with its use: spear, hunting knife, fish scalar, and ornamental. I counted seventy in all. Where in the world did he find these? I wondered. Bella Vista?

On the floor were huge chunks of crystal—maybe from the old Lodge that had burned a long time ago. He had onyx, too, probably from Hot Springs and several large rocks he'd labeled from our Sugar Creek that runs through Bella Vista Lake and spills on down for miles. On the window ledge he had logs with moss growing on them and a little pitcher of water to keep them wet.

At one end of the room was Joe's own private, tin-lined shower. I'd heard him singing in his loud warble and now I understood where that sound came from. Somehow I knew he wouldn't like us to see his shower and this part of his hideaway. I stood thinking of him in his tight jeans and big shirts with sleeves rolled up. Mrs. M had given Sally and me some of his old ones to wear over our clothes when we painted. Even though Joe was only a year and a half older than Sally, he was much taller. His wavy hair was thick like hers and he had one lock that always fell over his eye. He would sort of sling it out of the way with a shake of his head. His eyes were dark brown. It suddenly came to me that he'd be in the shower with no clothes on at all. Oh, my goodness.

I turned away so that I would start thinking about something else. I picked up a book off the table by his bed. It was a mystery. His bookshelves were loaded with books that fascinated me. I wanted to lie on his bed and read. I loved to read. Joe did too. It showed me a whole new side of him.

27

But Sally was calling me to help her strip the bed. "Strip the bed? Why? He'll know it was us won't he?" I asked her.

"Not when we get through with it," and she laughed like it was all so delicious to her. "I learned this in Camp Scott. It's called 'short-sheeting.' Come on. I'll show you. Fold the bottom one half way up and tuck it in. Then the top sheet goes on like usual. See? It covers up the dastardly deed. Put on the blanket and then when he jumps in bed and jams his feet down—they'll hit the short sheet. WHAM! They won't go down."

We stepped back when it was finished. You couldn't tell at all. I could just see Joe's face when he tried to push his big feet down and they wouldn't go but half way. I began to laugh but when I turned around, Sally was stuffing his pillowcase with rocks.

"Mikedosh, Sally, won't that hurt him?"

"Naww," we'll put the sharp ones on the bottom and just leave the little ones for his hard head to hit. He's going to love this."

"Love is hardly the word," I laughed.

When we got back upstairs we were so hungry. It was almost nine o'clock. We didn't even bother with cereal but began dropping bread into the toaster and when it popped up, we smeared it with big gobs of Hilda's pear honey. She made the best in the world. It was sweet and grainy and mixed with lots of butter on the toast, it tasted heavenly.

After about three apiece, we slowed down a bit. But we kept on toasting. I don't know exactly when the contest began. Each time one of us finished a slice, we stuck another in and pulled down the lever. We were tied when we finished the loaf. After a few seconds of silence, Sally marched into the kitchen and got a new loaf. We both began to grin—and to eat.

About the middle of the second loaf, we were both slowing way down. The pear honey and butter didn't taste so delicious any more. Each bite I chewed had trouble going down my throat. I noticed Sally having trouble swallowing, too, but we both kept on eating. Who wanted to be the first to give up?

I did. I ran to the bathroom fast. I knew I had lost, but I just couldn't help it. I felt sick, sick, sick! As my first upchuck hit into the potty, I realized I wasn't alone. Both of us knelt there and moaned and cried holding the rim on each side of the commode. Just when we'd think we

28

were through and would sit back to get a breath, more came rushing up and we had to lean over the toilet again. It was awful.

The next thing I knew, Mrs. M was bending over us holding a cold washrag on each of our foreheads. That felt so good. They'd been rained out of their fishing trip and had to come home early. It was nice to have her there and I felt comforted until I heard Joe laughing at us. This was not funny.

Strangely enough though, after we felt better and had confessed all we'd eaten and had listened to Mrs. M's warning to "Never do that again," Joe was nice. He called us out on the screened porch and played cards with us. He even taught me his special way to shuffle. You held half of the deck in each hand and tamped them down until the cards were perfectly even. Then you bent them, holding them with your thumb at the top and your pointy finger bent back to the knuckle to hold the middle part of the cards. You had to hold the bottom of the deck with your other fingers. After you bent them—you let go and they fluttered down together. It looked so professional. I did it over and over again after I finally got my hands to co-operate.

We sat there at the card table and played for hours with the rain pelting down on three sides of the screened porch. It washed the wind and everything smelled like honeysuckle and peppermint and it felt like we were wrapped in fragrant arms. Once in a while it blew mists through the screens and across the room but we were toasty warm in our jeans and sweaters. Hot tea and rice sweetened with sugar and a whiff of cinnamon comforted our tummies. Joe never said a teasing word. He was "almost human" as my mother sometimes said about people she didn't think much of.

Later, Sal and I crawled into our bed with extra quilts to keep away the night's chill. After we'd re-hashed the game and even laughed over the pear honey, we stopped talking. As I floated into sleep, I thought of Joe's short sheet and pillow filled with rocks. Had he gotten in bed yet? Right now I didn't feel so good about it. I got out of bed and went into the bathroom where the gas heater was lit. It was time to write about the day in my diary.

"…we both kept on eating. Who wanted to be the first to give up?"

When I got back in bed, I looked at Sally's face. She was still half-awake. "We haven't gone horseback riding yet—want to do that tomorrow?"

"Always, always" she said with sleepy sighs as she was sinking down into her pillow.

That was the last thing either of us said until morning.

Chapter 5

Horseback Riding

It was still dark when we started walking down the path the next morning. In the distance though, there was a rosy glow over the valley and I knew that on the other side of the dark hills it was already daylight. The air felt damp and cool and I wished it could stay this way all day long. It was shivery and exciting. We were on our way to fun. Sally began to skip so I knew she felt the same way I did. We skipped with our arms around each other until the hill was too uneven and steep.

Some people didn't like the smell of the stables. I'd seen them hold their noses and almost gag at the mixture of manure and trampled hay. But I'd grown up with it and the odors just went with all the rest: the fun of horses brushed 'till they shined, the smell of leather saddles and the strong coffee the guys boiled on a hot plate in the cow shed. Bessie, our Jersey cow ate there. One of the stable hands milked her in the summer when Daddy was so busy, then later he turned her out to pasture for the day. I went in and talked to her and I'm sure she knew me because she looked at me and swished her tail and sort of smiled as she chewed her cud.

Sally had her horse that she always rode, named Snip and my horse was Tony. Everyone knew us and let us put on our own saddles. Sally said it was because Daddy was their boss. He's not, really, but that made me feel good. The real reason was probably because she was a cottage owner's daughter and bought a season ticket to ride. Anyway—getting the horses ready ourselves took a lot less time than if they had done it for us.

We rode off and it wasn't even daylight yet. I led this time and took us up Lodge Hill because I had a surprise. Daddy had given me the key to one of the rooms that was still left standing after the Lodge burned. First, we got off our horses and tied them to a tree while we admired the tall crystal fireplace. It was the only part that didn't burn in the big lobby where a long time ago it was the center of attraction. In the first rays of sunlight the uneven edges of the glass rocks sparkled and danced for us.

We imagined with each other what it was like before. An old brochure I read at Uncle C. A.'s office had said that it "towered majestically over the main lobby."

"Let's play like we are sitting here on soft, cushy chairs sipping our Cokes and watching the fire flames and smelling the burning logs, okay?" Sally asked. I did for a little while but then urged her on to the secret room.

The key fit, even though the lock was still rusty, and we opened the door slowly, not sure what we'd find. Spider webs and boxes and chests covered in thick dust lined the walls. Hanging on the walls were faded paper flowers of red, purple, blue, and yellow. "What is this place?" Sally wanted to know. For an answer I pointed to several large posters showing pictures of the different times when the orchestra boys did their floorshows.

"Daddy said this was their prop room where they kept stuff for their acts," I told her. We opened one of the boxes and pulled out a long velvet cape—all full of holes—and some silky dresses, torn but gorgeous, with flounces and tight long sleeves.

One that I picked up simply fell apart into shreds in my hands. It was old and must have had what Mother would call dry rot. There were stacks of different hats some with tall straggly plumes, some with ratty fur, others with tassels, and one pointed like a dunce's cap. One large box had tattered clown costumes and big diapers with safety pins and a suit that resembled a monkey or maybe a gorilla.

We nearly choked on the dust, but it was such fun to dress up in them even if they were so fragile that bits of them kept tearing. Sally was a villain with a black hat and a mustache. She had me play the damsel in distress in a white dress that was almost black with dirt. She kept saying, "Who'll pay the rent?" in a deep voice and told me to act like I was crying. "It's called a melodrama. Our class went to see one at the high-school." Sally explained. She knows so much more about things than I do.

"Do you ever play dress-up in Tulsa," I asked.

"Sure, we get together and act out plays and make up stories. I think I'll go home and fix a costume box like this. Mother has some wigs and her old sequined evening dresses that she might give me. How about you? Do you play dress-up?"

"Who'll pay the rent?"

"I love to. My friends from town and I spend the night a lot with each other on the weekends. Especially at Jodee and Loudee's. And sometimes they come to my house and we sweep out one of the old deserted cottages and play like we're a family.

It's really fun to play at Aunt Ray and Uncle C. A.'s house. They would have us over before they leave for the winter, and she lets me go upstairs and try on her long dresses. Oh, and she has this fluffy boa made of ostrich feathers. Once she let me wear it and she gave me some old lipstick and mascara. You should have seen Daddy and Uncle C. A. I'd forgotten to loop the long skirt over my belt so my high heels got caught in it and I stumbled as I was making my entrance down the staircase. I fell the last three steps and landed right between them on the couch. I'll bet Daddy was embarrassed."

Sally laughed and dug into another box. There were gobs of necklaces made out of wooden beads of every color. We put millions of strings around our necks and immediately we were movie stars. She was Tallulah Bankhead and I was Veronica Lake. I pulled my hair over one eye like Veronica did. (I don't know how she could see anything.)

I guess we played a long time because when we heard the horses whinnying and peeked out the door, the sun was blaring down. It must be really late, I thought. "Quick, we gotta go, Sally. No tellin' how many customers have needed my horse." Both of us grabbed piles of props and stuffed them back into boxes and chests.

I worried all the way back thinking how Daddy wouldn't like this at all if he heard about it. We rode like crazy the last part when we got to the straight stretch. My stomach kept bothering me like I was real hungry. Both of us were off our horses at the same time and grabbed the brushes so we could cool them off.

The joke was on me. Boy was I relieved that it wasn't that late after all and almost no one had wanted to ride. The stable boys were playing cards on a rickety old table and hardly looked up at us.

"Well, lets just go out again this afternoon," Sally said.

"I just can't—I...." Actually, I felt like crying, I wasn't sure why. What I really wanted to do was to go sit on my rock up at Big Spring or to read or maybe write in my diary.

Sally came from around her horse and touched my hand. "That's okay." She smiled. "Let's go do something at the cabin. Maybe look at those new library books." It was as if she'd read my mind. We knew each other pretty well.

"Well," I struggled to think of something good to say back. Then it came to me, "Well, tomorrow is your day. You could choose for us to come ride horses again then."

"Sure," she said brightly. "Now—I'm starving. First one to the cabin has dibs on Hilda's cookies."

"Last one's a 'monkey's uncle'!" I screamed as I started out running.

We did read, after we washed the lunch dishes. Hilda was gone for a few days because her nephew was getting married in Tulsa. Sally washed and I dried and then we lay on the bed with *White Fang* for me and one of my Oz books for her. I must have fallen asleep a while and then waked up to pounding water in the bathtub. Must be a bubble bath, I thought. Lots of nights we took one together, sculpting each other's hair with bubbles and covering each part of our body with white foam. Still, it wasn't bedtime. Not even night yet.

Curious, I went into the bathroom rubbing the sleep from my eyes. There was Sally with a stack of different kinds of soap in a bowl beside her.

"It's an experiment," she explained, not looking up. "C'mon, help me. I'm trying to see which one of these gets hands the cleanest." With that, she began scrubbing with red Lifebuoy Soap under a full blast of water. "This one is supposed to be good for any kind of bacteria," she read on the label.

I picked up the Ivory—"99 and 44/100 Per Cent Pure—It Floats," I read, then lathered it up rubbing my hands hard. Next she tried Lava. "Gets The Greasiest Hands Clean." I switched to Palmolive, "The Soap Of Beautiful Women."

"Ya'll sure have a lot of different kinds of soap," I said, thinking how one kind did us at home. Then I remembered that Mother made our soap to wash our clothes. "My mother makes lye soap."

"Really?" Sally stopped to look up from her experiment. "How?"

"She puts grease in it, you know. All summer at the Pavilion, she saves the used grease from the kitchen. In the fall she boils it and adds lye and it stews until it turns white. You dip off the dark stuff from the top. I'm not sure if that's all she puts in. On washday, she builds a fire under the big black pot in the yard and when the water is steaming hot, she tosses in our clothes with a block of white lye soap and stirs 'em with a long clean stick. They come out so clean."

"That sounds like the hillbillies. Your mother isn't a hillbilly is she?" she picked up the green Palmolive and continued scrubbing her hands.

Of course Mother wasn't a hillbilly. I'd never thought of making lye soap as anything bad. I fished my soap out and rinsed my hands. All of a sudden they were stinging. They were dry and taut when I used the towel. I went in the other room and picked up my book and left Sally to finish the experiment.

I kept looking at my hands. They were swelling bigger and bigger. When Sally came in, we decided it must have been the soap. "Mikedosh, Connee, I'm so sorry they hurt. Mom's going to kill me."

"No. I wanted to do it. It's my fault."

Mrs. M called us in to help make sandwiches for supper. She looked at my red hands and gasped. "Connee, what in the world is wrong? Did you get stung?"

"No Ma'm," I answered, almost in tears. Even though Mother said always to tell the truth, I didn't want to get Sally in trouble, so I just said, "I guess I need some lotion." Both my hands were swollen and hurting. They itched but were also throbbing with pain.

Later, in bed, I dreaded tomorrow's horseback ride in the sun. This time, I didn't even want to write in my diary. My hands hurt too much. I just wanted to shut my eyes and go to sleep.

Chapter 6

Mumbo Jumbo

There wasn't any question about riding horses the next morning. My hands were still swollen and sore. Mrs. M. was mystified and I wasn't about to tell her what had caused the problem. She had me put a lot of lotion on them and then she wrapped them in clean cloths. Sally was sick over it and blamed herself—but I didn't. She chose that we stay home today and play games and just talk. That was fine with me. My head hurt a little but it was worth it to have conducted what Sally called our "Scientific Experiment With Well Known Brands of Hand Soap." She'd learned all about experiments in school. Now I knew about them, too. She showed me how to write up the results. We did a whole page on the "Unexpected Reaction of the Subject's Hands."

Mrs. M and Joe decided to check to see if the fish were biting in Bella Vista Lake. She didn't want to go very far away from us that day. That left us alone for a little while and we were glad. Just as Joe started down the steps, he called back, "Stay away from my room or you sneaky little girls will be very sorry." Then he laughed his silly laugh and leaped over the last five stairs making a perfect landing on the grass. "Sally—I've been to camp too, you know," he yelled. Then he shocked me. He said in a nice voice. "Bye Connee, take care of those hands," and hopped in the car, rolling his window up and looking straight ahead as they drove away.

Sally recovered first from his unusual behavior. "Let's go down and see if he left a booby-trap."

Before I could answer she looked at my hands and changed her mind. "Naw, let's make believe we are airline stewardesses and that the plane wrecked and we had to take care of two handsome college boys. See, they were hurt and we had to help them eat and bathe their feverish faces."

"And they liked us," I got into the story easily. "They told us that if we ever got back to civilization they wanted to date us." (My boyfriend was named Dave and he had black hair and was tall. Hers was named James Manuel and he had black hair too, but he also had a mustache.) It started raining and that made us hungry so we stopped; we raided the kitchen and ate some of the candy Hilda had hidden in the back of the cabinet. I stretched out on the foot of the bed with Kitty Thirteen—feeling a lot better—and Sally flipped on the radio.

She began to "swing and sway" with Sammy Kaye's orchestra. I watched from my curled up position on the bed, waiting because I knew she'd do something interesting. Sure enough, she began twirling the dial and reacting to the different announcers. One was selling Oxydol soap. She poured a whole imaginary box on her imaginary clothes and then put her hand up to her forehead in dismay that she had used so much. Next was a soap opera. She acted out one character then another in a dramatic love scene. Flipping the dial again, she sang the J-E-L-L-O theme song with them. Her voice trailed away as she went into the bathroom.

When she came back, Kitty Thirteen and I were playing tag under the covers. Outside it had begun to thunder and lightning. In between, I heard the beat of a bass drum and sat up. Sally was standing by the radio again. She put her finger to her lips and said, "Listen—I know this. It's a poem by Vachel Lindsay that we read in school:"

> *...Barrel-house kings, with feet unstable,*
> *Sagged and reeled and pounded on the*
> *table,*
> *Pounded on the table,*
> *Beat an empty barrel with the handle of a*
> *broom,*
> *Hard as they were able,*
> *Boom, boom, Boom,...*

The rhythm of the poem was beating-beating throughout the whole cottage. Sally had taken her daddy's cane and straw hat from the hat rack in the corner and was tapping and prancing in cadence with the words. The beating went on and on and I was almost hypnotized. The thunder and lightning had changed to a steady rain.

39

...THEN I had religion. THEN I had a vision.
I could not turn from their revel in derision.
THEN I SAW THE CONGO, CREEPING
    THROUGH THE BLACK,
CUTTING THROUGH THE JUNGLE
    WITH A GOLDEN TRACK.
Then along that river-bank
A thousand miles
Tattooed cannibals danced in files;
Then I heard the boom of the blood-lust
song
And a thigh-bone beating on a tin-pan
gong....

Sally marched into the kitchen, grabbed a pie pan and banged it with the cane.

...Listen to the creepy proclamation,
Blown through the lairs of the forest-nation,
Blown past the white-ants' hill of clay,
Blown past the marsh where the butterflies
play:-
"Be careful what you do,
Or Mumbo-jumbo, God of the Congo,
And all of the other

Gods of the Congo,
Mumbo-jumbo will hoo-doo you,
Mumbo-jumbo will hoo-doo you,
Mumbo-jumbo will hoo-doo you."

I was up there, now, parading along with Sally. She hopped on a chair. I hopped on one, too. She marched over the bed—I was right behind. She handed me a broom and I wrapped a dishtowel around my head with a flip.

40

*...And the gray sky opened like a new-rent
veil
And showed the apostles with their coats
of mail.
In bright white steel they were seated round
And their fire-eyes watched where the
Congo wound.
And the twelve apostles, from their thrones
on high,
Thrilled all the forest with their heavenly
cry:-*

Then came the finale and Sally and I were as much a part of it as if
we'd been right there. We jumped around stalking each other and keeping
time with our feet and our props.

*"Mumbo-jumbo will die in the jungle;
Never again will he hoo-doo you,
Never again will he hoo-doo you."...*

*...“Mumbo-jumbo is dead in the jungle.
Never again will he hoo-doo you,
Never again will he hoo-doo you.”*

The poem ended and the radio was silent but Sally and I kept repeating
it as we stomped one foot and then another and peered left and right:

“Never again will he hoo-doo you,
Never again will he hoo-doo you,
Never again will he....”

—and then we collapsed in laughter. The spell was broken. We were
breathless. It was wonderful. I couldn't believe it. We did it. It was
dancing and acting and not knowing what we were going to do next but
then knowing exactly what to do.

41

"Mumbo-jumbo will hoo-doo you, Mumbo-jumbo will hoo-doo you…"

A car drove up and two bedraggled fishermen got out. Their clothes were soaked with rain and their hats draped in scallops over wet hair. Mrs. M whistled up to us, and Joe ducked into his room. His shower started running even before she finished climbing the outside stairs. "Did you girls have a quiet, restful, rainy day?"

"Yes Ma'm," we answered in unison, crossing our fingers behind our backs.

Chapter 7

Mountain Climbers

"Are you sure your hands feel all right to ride horses?" Mrs. M wanted to know the next morning.

They still hurt a little, but I figured getting on Tony would help me forget how they itched. Besides, I didn't want to disappoint Sally and not ride again so I told her they were fine.

It was sprinkling a little but not enough to stop us. It made the air cool and welcoming. We felt pretty grown up when the stable boys told us to go on even though it might rain. They'd said, "Take on off. The horses know you and you know these hills as well as we do."

Sally carried a long rope around her saddle horn and I had a sack with two sandwiches, a jar of water, two apples and a surprise—a couple of Snickers that Mother had given me when I stopped by for clean clothes a week ago. We took the trails up above Lodge Hill. This time we didn't stop at the old Lodge, but as we rode along, I told her stories about when my cousin, Audrey Robbins ran the newsstand as a teenager. We thought that would be fun.

The ground was a little soft so we just poked along. Every once in a while we brushed against some limbs that grew close to the road and got showers of water from the leaves. As the sun came up, it shimmered through the branches and looked like rays from heaven. I wondered if heaven looked like this. Sally said it reminded her of places on other planets in the Saturday serials of Buck Rogers at the picture show.

Pretty soon, we came to a narrower part where we were really close to the edge of the hill. Sally stopped and tied Snip's reins to a tree away from the drop off and that's when I found out why she'd brought a rope. "See, we'll play like we are mountain climbers," she explained, and she talked fast like she would when she was pretending.

"The horses know you and you know these hills as well as they do."

I slid off Tony, tied him up and joined her where she was making a Girl Scout knot in the end of the rope so it would be real tight and secure. I checked the tree she tied it to and made sure it wouldn't pull up by its roots. "I didn't know you knew how to tie knots like that," I told her.

"To be sure, I am an official Girl Scout of America," she said in a solemn voice. "Remember my good friend, Mary Grace? She and I and a whole bunch of girls went to Camp Scott. There was a charming leader. She was a police officer and weighed about six hundred pounds. She was always threatening us and we were such good girls, I can't see why."

"You never played pranks?"

"Me? You're asking me if I ever played pranks? You hurt my feelings, my dear. All I did last year was to organize a midnight party to celebrate when our cabin won the canoe race. Of course, with lights out at ten p.m. it was a challenge. Can I help it if we were creative and decided to raid the icebox when we ran out of food?"

"Mary Grace told me that when you went to camp with her you taught her to swim."

"She did?"

"You bet. She said when she told you that she just didn't have the nerve to go in the deep end, you gave her a *gentle* push, right into the ten feet end of the pool!"

"Well she paddled out." Sally said innocently.

"Yes, she said she had to swim or drown."

"So, she learned to swim," we said in unison.

"Secretly we all loved Camp Scott," Sally said with a fake grimace. "It was so horrible that it was wonderful—to face it together. Survivors get real close to each other, you know."

For the next half-hour we climbed down and back up "Mt. Everest." Sally told me that it's one of the highest mountains in the world. I got us some sharp sticks and we played like they were the picks that you jam into the side of the mountain to make something to hold on to when you're real mountain climbers.

Sally went to a lot of picture shows in Tulsa. She told me about one that had this guy in it who died trying to reach the top of the peak. They had a lot of trouble getting his body back down. That was a scary thought.

She said she'd hold onto the rope and I could go first. I looked at the solid rock cliff between the ground and me and wondered how I'd get a toehold. It was so far. What if I'd fall?

46

"Sally," I said, "How far do you think it is, anyhow?" I wanted to do it, but right now I was feeling a little unsure.

"Oh, I don't know. My rope is fifty feet long and, let's see, take away the part where I wrapped it around the tree and the knot and there's some left over—I guess it's 35 feet down to the bottom?"

I didn't want to ruin our adventure, so I shut my eyes and started down, holding the rope tightly with my hands and wrapping my legs around it. It wasn't so bad. Sort of like the rope we climbed in Physical Education, at school.

But then the rope began to hurt. My hands stung so much it brought tears. I opened my eyes and looked down. "Oh, mikedosh," I yelled. It still looked like miles to the bottom. But I had to go on. I closed my eyes, moved down several more times and opened them again. Horrified, I saw that some of the blisters had burst on my hands and were oozing down my arm. Some of them were bleeding. I let go of the rope.

I hit with a thud. As soon as I got my breath, though, I realized that I was fine. The ground was soft and muddy from the rains and I hadn't fallen far. I looked up at Sally and laughed. I wasn't hurt much, just shaken up. I'd done it! I hollered up, "Yoo-hoo, come on in—the water's fine."

Sally made it down with no trouble. I don't know if she was scared. Her face sure was red though.

We wrapped her handkerchief and mine around my hands. Thankfully, Sally went first. I hated the idea of climbing back up, but it turned out to be easier than coming down. There were more ledges to put your feet on than I had thought and by leaning back on the rope we both went up pretty fast.

We were starved. When we saw how high the sun was, we decided it must be time to eat our lunch. I poured my water on the handkerchiefs and it soothed my hands.

Afterward, we rode on around Skyline Drive. The horses were rested and wanted to trot but we slowed down to read the names on the carports. We passed "The Glad Shack," where the mother was named Gladys, "Trails End," "Just Loafin'," and "Top of The World." That one had wooden steps that started way down in the valley and were built all the way up the hill to the front door of the cottage.

Next, we rode by "Fellows Nest." It belonged to a famous poet named Uncle Henry Fellows. Well, anyhow, my cousin Ima Lou May called him

Uncle. She and her mother and daddy got to be good friends with him when they ran a grocery store at Bella Vista. They said he was well known in Chicago and lots of big places. That's why it was so special that he wrote a poem about Ima Lou. The Bella Vista Breezes newspaper was always printing stories about him.

We were lucky. He was sitting on his porch swing with a tablet in his lap. Sally just knew he'd invite us in for lemonade and give us his autograph; maybe even write a poem about us. But he barely smiled—just kept on writing. "I think he looks so distinguished with his curly hair and mustache," she whispered.

"Maybe next time he won't be busy," I said.

"Maybe next time we'll go up and tell him we're interested in publishing a poem," she plotted.

When we got back down the hill, the horses picked up speed. "Let's gallop down Tulsa Row before we take them back," I suggested. I didn't have to say it twice. She raced away on Snip. The road was smooth and level, a great place to end a ride. Sal and Snip got to the turnaround first, but I caught up and we raced like the wind side by side all the way back by the Pavilion. When we got close to the stables we got off and walked the horses to cool them down. Not until I began brushing Tony did I feel my hands stinging again.

Chapter 8

The Cave

We had started to the Plunge to swim when I saw Daddy drive up in our Chevy instead of his little coupe. He honked at us and pulled right up to where we were.

"Hi, honey. You girls look like you're on your way for a swim. Would you like to go with me to wash the car first?"

"Would you?" I asked Sally, hoping she'd say yes.

"Sure, can we help? We've got our bathing suits on."

"That's exactly what I wanted you to say. Hop in girls."

I wondered why Daddy was taking time out to do this in the middle of the day. Wasn't he working? He explained before I could ask: "C. A. has a big group coming in on the train into Rogers and we'll need extra cars to pick them up. We'll wash this and then W. T. can drive it to help bring them here."

Sally's eyes flashed, she was up to something. Some of the straws were coming loose at the edge of her hat and I watched her pull at them. Mikedosh. She was unraveling the whole brim. She kept on loosening the strands until there was nothing left but a feathery fringe. It looked so cute that by the time we got to Sugar Creek, I had mine unraveled, too. We put them on and grinned at each other.

Daddy drove out into the water onto a flat rock where people had been washing their cars all my life. "Let me get started and then I'll call you when I'm ready for some help," he told us.

We waded down the creek to keep cool. A man who knew Daddy took a picture of us as we pranced like majorettes in our hats and our look-alike shorts that Mother had made for us.

When Daddy whistled, we stripped off our clothes to our swimsuits. He gave us a bucket to dip up the water from the flowing creek onto the car and we soaped it all over. Then we climbed up on the running boards and poured water over the roof to rinse it well. Daddy had already cleaned the tires and the creek swished the soapsuds away. He then dried the whole car with a chamois skin. All three of us shined it with old rags and stepped back to admire how clean it looked. I gave Sally a push and she sat down with a splat in the creek. As she was falling though, she grabbed my leg and pulled me down with her. Daddy gave us about two minutes to splash each other before he started the motor.

"Where are you going now, Daddy?" I asked, wanting to be around him some more. I was careful to put the endings on my words. Daddy came from a real country background where they said "ain't" for aren't, "crik" for creek, and "you-uns" for you. He learned to speak correctly from Uncle C. A. and from the people who came to the resort. It was very important to him that I speak right too.

Sometimes I forgot and he told me, "Honey it is important how you talk. You are neither above nor below any of these people who come here, but if you don't use the right words, they won't know that." Mother said Daddy was a self-made man. He left home when he was only twelve and joined the Hila Morgan Show. That was a traveling group that put on plays for small towns. He helped them put up and take down the stage and he said that he learned a lot about stuff he'd never heard of way back in Cave Creek, Arkansas. He sent money back to his mother and brothers and her two little orphaned grandchildren she was raising. (He'd say the right word was "rearing.") He read my schoolbooks each year on the first day I brought them home in the fall and said he would keep on studying even while I was going through college.

Another thing he kept saying to me was to "Always do your part." I think that's why he kept doing stuff for the Matofskys. He didn't want us not to do our part. I was hoping we could be with him some more and was I tickled when he said, "I'm headed up to Wonderland Cave as soon as I take the car back to your brother. Maybe you two would like to go with me and then I can drop you back at the pool later?"

"Are we going to get to ride in your coupe, Mr. May?" Sally asked.

"If you don't mind riding in the rumble seat," Daddy answered, smiling because he knew that was just what she wanted.

The experience was dusty, dust in our mouths and dust in our eyes as Daddy sped up Cave Hill. But we both loved waving at people who turned to stare at us riding in the little seat outside the back of the car.

We climbed out and ran to the entrance of the Cave. No need for tickets since we weren't sightseers.

50

"All three of us shined it with old rags and stepped back to admire how clean it looked."

"I'm going on down to see how the men are coming along with the blow torches, girls. Come on down when you are ready."

Sal and I didn't try to keep up with him. We stopped and looked at the water dripping off the ceiling, and the bat droppings and the little alcove that was behind bars. That was where they aged the wine that they made in the Winery.

"Now, didn't Mr. Linebarger get your daddy to help do this underground nightclub?"

"Yes," I answered proudly. "Uncle C. A. was in Paris and he saw one that was not nearly as big as this. He asked Daddy to get some men and start getting it ready to be a nightclub. That was 1929, the year I was born, AND he sent a wire that same year. A real telegram. The Linebargers were on a boat on Lake Constance and had just visited on The Isle of Manau—that means May Island. So he sent this wire saying: "Name The Girl Constance.""

"And your real name is Constance Virginia May."

"Right. Just like your real name is Roseanne Matofsky. And the cottage is named the "Joe-Anne" after you and Joe. Now, why did they nickname you Sally?"

"Because, my lovely Connee, Joe is only a year and a half older than me and he couldn't say Sister plainly. In Tulsa, where I grew up, everyone calls me Roseanne. Only my family calls me Sally."

"Oh." I said. Then thought to myself how lucky I was that I got to call her Sally.

"Do you ever come to dances down here?" she wanted to know.

"Not much. Daddy says they are a little too wild. People drink a lot. But last summer when Mother fired my nighttime sitter—you know, before I came and stayed with you, I was only eleven but they brought me up here to the cave on Saturday and Sunday nights."

"What was it like?"

"Oh, elegant! Women in taffeta or organdy evening dresses. They rustled when they walked by me. Mother was a hostess that weekend. Sometimes, she waits on tables and wears an ugly green uniform and keeps the other waitresses busy, but that night she had on her heavenly blue chiffon. She looked so pretty. Daddy always wears a suit and they danced once and I loved watching them. The acoustics are great down here, too. I got to sit near the band and it made them sound like they had thirty instruments."

"Mother was a hostess…, Daddy always wore a suit…"

"Remember too, Sally—the picture post cards of the Tom Thumb Wedding? I came to that. All the little kids were dressed up like grown ups. Joe Applegate was the preacher. W. T was the groom and Helen Ruth Haxton, the bride. Betty Ivy and I were flower girls. And another time, we got to see the Arkansas Senate when it met down here."

Daddy was showing the men how to put away the blowtorch that dried out the wooden dance floor. "You can spread out the Spangles, if you want to" he told us.

We shook the shiny flakes all over the big room, then skated and slid around to prove how slick it would make it for the dancers. Sally thought it would be funny if one of them would fall and her dress would go over her head.

She got behind the long white marble counter and played like she was serving me a pop. I could see both of us in the big bar mirror. We were framed in gold and I had her turn around and look, too. Then we checked out the Orchestra Boys' pit where they played swing music. I told her I'd had a crush on the piano player with the cute name Harley Haley ever since they got off the bus that first day of the season.

"I like Dave, the one who plays trumpet," she whispered. "He's only sixteen. I'm glad they stay the whole summer." I sat at the piano and she sat where Dave sits. It was so romantic.

All around the room there were two levels of rock tables in booths with soft lighting. We sat in one and the rock walls were about as high as our shoulders. They were jagged and made of beautiful stone. Some had a few crystals. We had to snuggle close to each other because it was drippy, damp, and cold. "You know, they say that one time Jessie James used this for his hideout and then escaped through the other entrance into Missouri," I said.

"No kidding? Maybe that's why they made the movie about him at Pineville, since it's only a few miles from here. Remember the summer your grandmother came to visit and she heard that 'Pretty Boy' Floyd, was alive and hiding here and she kept a baseball bat under her bed?" Sally asked. We snickered at that.

"What does your daddy do at the cave?

"He keeps bad things from happening," I answered. He carries a blackjack in his pocket in case any of the University crowd gets rowdy. He lets everyone know he expects them to act like ladies and gentlemen, especially if they try to smash their glasses on the rocks or go beyond the point where the cave is lighted and explored. There are a lot of deep drop offs back there."

"I think I like the Pavilion better," Sally said. "The ballroom has so much fresh air and children can come, too."

"Still, Uncle C. A. had a great idea making this," I said, wanting to be loyal. "It's in Ripley's 'Believe It Or Not,' you know."

"Of course, Bird Brain—it's on the sign outside. 'World's largest Underground Night Club,' right?"

"Okay, Miss Smarty Pants—race you back up to the top and we'll see." And I took off running.

We ran almost halfway on the wet path then doubled over out of breath. It was a long climb the rest of the way, up the stairs. We came out into the bright daylight and hot air and I shut my eyes and sat down. Sally was reading the sign when Daddy came out and said it was time to go.

Sally had wanted to hike up to Devil's Hole since we were so near to it. It was just across the road and up the hill. I had to admit it was always a spooky—fun feeling to look down into that dark place. It was like a cave that went straight up and down instead of being a room you could walk in. Once when W. T. was little, his little dog dug out a place under the fence in our yard. W. T. followed him through the opening and all the way up Cave Hill. Whole bunches of people were out searching for him and were they scared when they found him and his little dog right at the edge of Devil's Hole.

So, I said I would go. Secretly, though, I wanted to be with Daddy some more.

"Daddy, how long will it be before I can work in Wonderland Cave?" I asked.

"Not for a long time, Honey," he smiled, getting into the coupe.

Impulsively I leaned into his window and kissed his whiskery face. He looked surprised and smiled a shy smile then sped away, spinning the rocks and stirring up the dust. I stood there thinking: my daddy will need to shave before the dance tonight at the cave.

Dear Diary,

It was so much fun today to see Daddy. I liked telling Sally about him. When we were at Devil's Hole we threw rocks down. They must have gone for miles because we never heard them land. Then she told me her mother and daddy wished Uncle C. A. wouldn't make all of us work so hard (only she called him Mr. Linebarger). She just doesn't understand how we all love to work. Still, I heard Mother arguing with

Daddy about it last winter. When Japan started the war on Pearl Harbor Day, she wanted him to go work in a defense plant. She said the Linebargers just didn't know Daddy was worth so much. My daddy yelled at her at first and made her cry. Then he told her that he didn't want to live away from all of us. Besides, he just couldn't do that to Uncle C. A. because the resort needed him. Then he got real quiet and told Mother that C. A. was like the father he'd never had. I sure didn't want Daddy to leave. I know Mother would miss him, and I don't see him enough as it is. Well, good night Mother and Daddy and W. T. and God and Sally. I love you dear sweet diary. Sorry I don't write more often.

Connee

Chapter 9

The Birthday Party

This was one day when neither Sally nor I needed to decide what we'd do. Julia Ann Paisley had invited us to her cottage for her birthday party. We woke up early, grinned at each other, sat on each side of the bed and slipped our feet into house shoes then hand in hand tip-toed out to the screened porch without anyone hearing us. I was so eager that my fingers were clumsy as I tried to wrap my present. Sally had trouble, too. Her paper just wouldn't fit her gift. She kept cutting it smaller and smaller. I was giving my favorite present: paper dolls. There was a figure of Shirley Temple and her complete wardrobe for dancing and there were swimming outfits and lots of play clothes. I loved the long, silky blue pajamas with a matching robe and house shoes.

Joe came up the stairs letting the screened door slam. He picked up my gift before I could stop him.

"Well, what have we here? 'Little girlees' paper dolls."

"Give me those," I demanded. I grabbed at them but he lifted them above his head. "C'mon, Joe. I have to wrap that right now."

"Oh, she's in such a hurry to get to the little girlees' party. Here, little girl. Here are your nice paper dollies." He tossed them on the table in front of me, shrugged his shoulders and went in to find some food.

Sally wadded up and threw away her paper that had Happy Birthday written all over it with hilarious pictures of The Katzenjammer Kids from the funny papers. She spread out a new sheet on the card table. "When did you get the paper dolls?"

"I caught a ride in to Bentonville yesterday while you were with your mother at the dentist's office in Rogers."

"Did you know the people in the car?"

I think she was amazed that I hitchhiked. She says they can't do that in Tulsa. So, it was fun to say kind of casual like "Oh, it was a family from Chicago."

Sure enough, she was quiet and just sat there thinking about that while I got the corners taped on my package. Then she smiled and said, "You sure are lucky."

I was so proud there was something that I could do that impressed Sally. Suddenly, a saying of Grandmother's popped into my mind. When I felt like that I could do something better than someone else, she looked at me through her little round glasses. (I think she saw me better than I could see myself.) Then she would say: "Don't forget Connee, 'Pride goes before a fall'!" A little shiver ran through me. Maybe I was going to have something bad happen—something embarrassing that would be my "fall."

"Come on, beautiful Connee—we have lots of hours before the party. Want to play Rummy? Blackjack? Battle?"

We played all three and ate vegetables for lunch because Mrs. M insisted, then we took a rest and finally it was nearly two-thirty. Time to go.

Mrs. M let Joe drive part of the way. I was only eleven when Daddy taught me last year. I'm better at it than Joe. I sure wouldn't want to drive the Matofsky's car though. Mrs. M is always telling him to "Look out—or watch what you're doing!" They changed drivers when they got to the curvy roads. "Thank goodness." I thought.

Julia Ann lived on Lodge Hill right above Tulsa Row. It was one of the nicer cottages. A big rustic sign said PAISLEY right above the carport and inside they had created sort of a playroom. Their real home was in Little Rock where Julia Ann's father owned a drug store. He couldn't come to spend the whole season but had come just for the party. The rest of them, including Julia Ann's Grandmother got to stay all summer at Bella Vista where there were cool breezes and the nights were perfect for sleeping. Like the rest of the owners—they looked for "Whitey," my daddy, to find out if everything like water and electricity were fixed up and to see if there had been any break-ins in the nine months that they'd been away.

Mrs. Paisley had decorated the carport for our party and there was a table all set up for refreshments. We knew those always came last so we piled our gifts by the tall glass pitcher of lemonade. Sally and I took a quick peek at the huge cake with a big 13 decorated with dozens of yellow icing roses that matched the lemonade.

There were twelve of us—thirteen counting Julia Ann. Mrs. Paisley made a game of having us tell about the different places we lived. There were some from Saint Louis, Baton Rouge, Jackson, Mississippi, Oklahoma City, Kansas City, and several from Tulsa—including Sally. Then there were the Arkansawyers: Julia Ann and me. I felt glad that I was from the same state as the birthday girl.

Julia Ann was someone I really liked. She had golden curly hair, a smile that never stopped, and she was so friendly and sweet to everyone. I felt almost as good in her home as I did in Sally's. Daddy and Mother were friends with all the cottage owners, it didn't matter how wealthy they were and Julia Ann let me know that she was a good friend, too.

The floor of the carport was plenty wide enough for the special activity Mrs. Paisley had planned. "I know that each of you has a talent," She told us. "Don't you think it would be fun to take turns and perform for each other?"

This made my stomach feel empty and my throat tight. Usually I loved to play games if I already knew what the rules were. But talent? What talent did I have? I couldn't think of a thing except being a good worker. That's not what she meant, though. She meant singing, or ballet, or telling jokes. Oh, good heavens! I wished I could slip out of the back door. Mrs. Paisley was talking: "And to warm us up—why don't we sing with the Victrola? Do you all know "You Must Have Been A Beautiful Baby?" I did! I sang out with the group and it really sounded good. We sang it over at least three times getting louder as we went:

"When you were only startin' to go to kindergarten, I'll bet you drove the little boys wild. And when it came to winnin' blue ribbons, I'll bet you showed the other kids how. I can see the judge's eyes as he handed you the prize. I'll bet you made the cutest bow. Oh you must have been a beau-ti-ful baaaabeee, 'cause baby, look at you now!"—We shouted the ending and several took a bow.

"Now who's going to be first?" I started moving to the back of the group. I was thinking so much about how I felt that it was a minute before I realized that Sally was already up front. She did a clever reading. Those were poems or stories you learned from special teachers outside school. I knew because mother saved her butter and eggs money each fall so she could give me "Expression" lessons. My mind wandered a little and I

59

could just see her squeezing the butter in the butter mold until there wasn't a drop of water in it. Women stood in line to get Gladys May's butter. They said it was so firm and delicious.

Sally finished the last line. We clapped and clapped and she curtseyed as if she'd been on stage all her life.

Why wouldn't one of my Expression pieces come to me? My mind was a blank. How had Sal remembered that long poem so well? It was as if she'd been planning it all week.

Another girl did a song. It was pretty good. Then someone did cartwheels. Mrs. Paisley had us all stand back so she'd have plenty of room. The applause was what did it. I kept hearing the applause and even though my face was red, I knew it was time for me to perform.

I raised my hand and told them I'd do a tap dance. Julia Ann put the record on for me. "You Must Have Been A Beautiful Baby." My feet began to move and it was heaven. I swung my hands and shuffled and tapped and thought of Fred Astaire. Up and down the room I danced and once I jumped up on a chair and kept on moving my feet to the rhythm. It was giddy. It was electric. They loved me. I loved me. The applause at the end made me curtsey, too. I was so proud.

My piece of chocolate cake had part of the 13 on it. Just think. I'd be a teenager this November. Sally had had her thirteenth on March 21st, the first day of spring. This fall we'd be the same age again. There was my favorite—tooti-fruity ice cream with lots of cherries, nuts and bits of something green, and all kinds of goodies in it. What could be better? We laughed and ate with our mouths full and giggled when the lemonade drooled down our chins and forgot that we were almost young ladies. Julia Ann opened all her presents. Sally had given her a bright red autograph book and we all got to write verses in it. When Julia Ann opened her paper dolls, Joe's teasing came to me and I had a funny feeling. Maybe she felt too old to play with them. After all, she was a teen-ager now. But she gave me a big smile and said "Thank You."

How I wished later that my happiness could have lasted. One of the girls from Baton Rouge was helping hand out the balloons that were for each of us. As she handed me mine, it accidentally burst. She jumped— then she said in her Louisiana drawl, "Connee—do you all think you will evah get to take lessons and learn how to do a real tap-dance?" I don't think anyone heard her but me. I prayed not.

What a fool I had made of myself. I hadn't been tap-dancing at all. There were lessons you had to take to do that. My face flared with heat. Oh, how embarrassing. What a dummy I'd been. How proud. "Pride goeth before a fall" Oh, Grandmother! Why had I danced? Then I looked at Sally. Of course she knew about steps for tap dancing. No doubt she was embarrassed too, and maybe she wished she weren't my closest friend anymore. And Julia Ann. Had I ruined her party? I'd never get in front of a crowd again. Never would I let myself feel this bad again.

Suddenly, I knew what I must do. Mrs. Paisley was right by me, so I thanked her for the party and told her I needed to leave early. She asked me if I was sure I didn't want to wait to walk with Sally, and I told her, "Yes Ma'm, I'm sure." I turned and went as fast as I could out the door kind of yellin' back at Julia Ann: "I had a good time." I hadn't forgotten how to be polite. Sally didn't have a chance to ask me where I was going.

"I swung my hands…and thought of Fred Astaire."

Chapter 10

Alone

When I got out of sight, I began to run. I wanted to get away as far as I could. Pretty soon I was out of breath and slowed to a walk. It was so hot my party dress was suffocating. Its high neck scratched me and I could feel the perspiration running down and making circles under my arms below the puffed sleeves. I hated puffed sleeves. Why did Mother have to make them? They stood up like I was still a little girl. I'll bet I looked like a silly little girl making believe I could tap dance—and didn't I know that only little girls played with paper dolls. Oh, why didn't I get a more grownup gift? I guessed that Julia Ann would give them to her little sister. She'd tell her she was thirteen. Too old for kid stuff.

I was coming down Lodge Hill. I sure didn't want to go back to the cottage. I needed to be alone. I'd go home. That's where I wanted to be, home.

The front door of our house was locked but when I went around to the back, it was open. Closing the door behind me I looked around at my home. It felt so good. So safe. I went straight to my bedroom and pulled the cardboard boxes out from under my bed. Taking the lid off of the first one, I lifted out a paper doll and stared at the extra hand on its shoulder. Funny, when I'd first begun cutting the figures out of catalogs, it upset me that there was always a spare arm or leg overlapping the person I wanted to have in my collection. It was impossible to cut it away without losing part of the doll that I wanted. Now I realized that as I'd played with them, I never noticed those extra parts any more. This one I had named Lana, after Lana Turner, the movie star. To make the dolls less flimsy, I'd made flour and water into paste, stuck them on cardboard that came out of the candy boxes at the Pavilion, then carefully cut them out.

In the other box were the store bought paper dolls Mother had given me for birthdays or Christmas. There were Jane Withers, Alice Faye and

Betty Grable, showing her famous legs. They were better made but I didn't love them a bit more than the ones from the catalog.

I put the lids back, tucked the boxes under my arm and went to the kitchen. Grabbing a handful of wooden matches from the metal holder nailed above the kitchen stove, I took the shoe boxes outside where we had scooped out a place for campfires and put a ring of rocks around it to keep it from catching the woods on fire behind our house. It wasn't very dangerous because there wasn't much grass. I could just hear Mother saying; "This dirt isn't good for anything except for chickens to scratch in." Remembering it made me laugh, but then I started to cry.

I gathered some kindling—little sticks that were everywhere on the hillside—and made a tepee of them inside the ring. The wood was so dry that when I added a few leaves and struck the first match, the fire crackled into action. I set the boxes down, took off each lid and knelt on the ground to see the contents. One by one, I lifted each of my dear dolls out, called it by name and then kissed it goodbye before I dropped it into the eager flames.

"I …kissed it goodbye before I dropped it into the eager flames."

Chapter 11

Gone

When I got back to the Matofsky's cabin, everyone was on the front porch stoop, waiting. Surely they didn't know what I'd done? Usually Mrs. M was back in her bedroom reading or in the pool doing her famous backstroke. Joe was almost always down in his room puttering around and Mr. Matofsky? Well—Mr. Matofsky was always either out on a walk or standing on the little stoop at the head of the steps looking down at the lake. Today though, they were all there, even Hilda. It was a little crowded. Their faces, all turned toward me as I came up the trail—looked really serious. I knew something was terribly wrong!

Mrs. M had us all go in and sit down in the screened porch. I was really getting scared. Maybe something had happened to one of my family. Daddy always drove a little too fast and Mother worked so many long hours and W. T. might have had a wreck going in to Bentonville for groceries for the Pavilion and—I was imagining so much that I was actually relieved when Mrs. M said it was Kitty Thirteen.

Then I saw Sally's face. Her honey colored skin had turned to dark red. She was crying—her hands were squeezed into tight fists. She looked mad and she looked hurt. I'd never seen her this way before. She talked low and her lips were tight so that it was hard to understand her. "But how did she get hit by a car? You know she never leaves our cabin. Did one of you do it?"

"No, Sally dear," Mrs. M answered in a quiet voice. She touched Sally's shoulder. It looked like she wanted to put her arms around her, but she didn't. "But you know how sometimes people drive up to our carport thinking that the road goes on a lot farther? I guess your little kitty was such a tiny ball of fur that they didn't see her. Actually, I had just started down to get her. She was chasing a little yellow butterfly. She never knew what hit her."

"I knew something was terribly wrong!"

Mr. Matofsky came over and put his arm around Sally's shoulder. She leaned her head against him. This was really tough on Sally. I had had so many kitties and it broke my heart when one of them was sick or killed by some animal. But Ol' Winery was the only one that always stuck in my mind. I'd had her lots of years and we'd only had Kitty Thirteen for a few weeks.

"You both loved her so much. We had all grown to love her." Mrs. M. said gently. I thought about how nice she was being. Nicer than I had ever seen her. "Bless her heart, she had bloomed out to be such a pretty one, her coat all grown out and her eyes bright…."

"She's really dead this time, isn't she Mom?" Sally sobbed. She ran into her bedroom and I followed. Joe and Hilda started after us, but Mrs. M shook her head.

I shut the bedroom door and lay down beside her. She cried so hard. I put my arm around her wishing I could help. We stayed that way a long time until she heard a noise and sat up.

Joe was knocking on the door instead of barging in. That was a surprise, and his voice sounded nice too. "Hey Sister and Connee. Mom wants to know if you want me to bury your cat?" We didn't answer so he said something more like himself. "Unless you want to look at her poor little mangled body?"

Sally threw her pillow at the door. "No, Beetle Brain! We'll bury her ourselves. Don't you touch her!"

"Okay, okay. Don't get so riled. I'm going to take the dogs for a walk. GOODBYE."

Mrs. M was right behind him. She came in and sat on the bed. That was unusual. "Now girls, it's going to be dark soon and I don't want you out trying to bury your Kitty tonight. And don't pay any attention to Joe. I'm positive it was over in a hurry and she didn't know she was hit. I brushed her hair and she looks just like she's asleep."

"Where is she?" Sally wanted to know.

"Well, I put her in a nice box, but first I put her little blanket in and laid her on it and then covered her up."

When she told us that, my chest began to feel like a big heavy person was sitting on it. The picture in my mind of Kitty Thirteen wrapped in her little blanket made it seem so real.

We hardly said a word as we got ready for bed that night. After I thought Sal was sound asleep I heard her soft crying. I took hold of her hand and lay there thinking of how every night, Kitty Thirteen would nibble my chin and put her little paw on my cheek. She'd go from one of us to the other and then finally curl up between us after giving herself a bath all over with her tiny pink tongue. I guessed she was a Kitty I'd never forget. How could I forget her? I cried, too.

In my dreams, someone kept calling my name. There was a big fire. Someone I couldn't see was getting too close to it but I couldn't stop the person. Then, a hand on my shoulder and my name again. It was Sally.

"Wake up, Connee. You're having a bad dream."

I opened my eyes and I was at the cottage. There was Sally. She was up on her elbow looking into my face with concern. I told her I was awake and okay now.

She sank back down on the bed and I thought she went back to sleep. Then she was up on her elbow again. "Where did you go today after the birthday party?" she frowned as if she were accusing me. "Julia Ann couldn't find you and neither could I. She wanted to thank you and tell you that your paper dolls were her most favorite gift." Sally didn't wait for an answer but lay her head down and immediately went back to sleep. Maybe I'd explain, later. Right now, I had to think some more....

Chapter 12

The Burial

In the morning, Sally chose the place where we would dig. I thought it was fitting that it was by the creek where we'd first found Kitty Thirteen. Each of us had a small garden spade but the ground was so hard and had so many rocks that it was a long time before we could get the hole big enough for the shoebox. Before we had left home we'd brushed Kitty's hair with her own brush. Sally put her blue blanket down and I laid her on it then we both cried again when I covered her and put the lid on the box.

Once the box was in the grave, we sprinkled it with wild flowers. I got two sticks and made a cross. Sally fastened it with the rubber band off my ponytail and stuck it in some of the dirt we'd managed to pile on after we put the little coffin in the grave. "Ashes to ashes and dust to dust," quoted Sally. I didn't much like that but she said it so solemnly I figured it was okay. I thought about singing a hymn but Sally took off running—sort of like she did that first day when she dipped Kitty Thirteen into the icy water and thought she was dead. But this time, Sally ran toward the Big Spring. This time Mrs. M wouldn't be able to revive Kitty Thirteen in front of the gas stove. This time she really was dead.

As we got near the spring, you could hear the "kaboom, kaboom" of the rams Daddy had installed a few years before to compress the water and pump it up to the cottages. The sound of their rhythm comforted me. We went over and sat under the big rock overhang where the spring came out in a pipe so that it was easier to get a drink. We put our hands under the chilly water and splashed a little on our faces and eyes. It felt good after crying.

As if we'd already talked about it, we began to climb Spring Hill. It took lots of concentration because if you didn't put your feet in a secure spot, the loose rocks would cause you to slide and fall. I'd showed Sally several summers before how to turn each foot sideways and to lean over toward the steep hill to keep your balance. Today, she shinnied up as easily as my grandmother's goat climbed a fence. At the fork, I kept left of the huge rock boulder that divided the two trails. It wasn't a day to climb Fat Man's Squeeze. Like its name, it was the narrower side, with several spots that were hard to climb because there was nothing but solid rock. The left trail was narrow too, but through the years, the ground had eroded the dirt and exposed the scraggly tree roots. You could grab hold of them like a staircase rail to help yourself up. My feet knew every familiar foothold. After all, I'd climbed there at least a million times.

Ever since I can remember, this had been my rock. It was gigantic; its base came almost down to Big Spring. The top was solid but had several ledges jutting out from it. It was dangerous to go too far out, so we sat on the first ledge and looked way down at the overhang to Big Spring. Columbine clung to it and hung down in vines of brown and yellow-orange flowers. The wind blew our hair back from our faces and we breathed in its sweet, clean smell. As we listened to the rushing sound of the spring and the "kaboom" of the rams far below, Sally stretched her arms toward the cottages sprinkled on the far away hills and said, "Oh, it's heavenly up here on Inspiration Point."

Even though everyone else called it Inspiration Point, I'd told her that when she and all the rest go back to the cities, this was my hideaway. No one else in the world understood exactly what it meant to me. Mother and Daddy knew that I climbed up here, but they didn't know that it was when I was hurting because Daddy got mad at Mother or disappointed in myself or happy or when I just want to be alone to think.

We fell down exhausted, and I began doing what I always did—sweeping the little rocks off each ledge with my hands. There were little tufts of silky green grass springing up in the crevices, making it soft to lie on once the rocks and sticks were gone.

It felt so right here. Sally lay on her tummy beside me and we were still for a long time. The morning sun felt comforting like it feels in a warm bath. Sally had her head down on her arms and without looking up she asked me, "Where do you think things go when they die?"

"Well—my grandmother says that we'll all see each other in heaven. When she says that, I think inside me that I'll see my pets there, too. I sure hope so."

We were quiet again and a redbird began trilling his call. I remembered learning that they sang at the four corners of their territory morning and evening. I was glad they claimed this spot, too. I sat there wanting to tell her more about how I pray. It was the only secret left. She knew everything else about me now:—the ones I liked at school—the teacher that was mean to me and the rest that were so good and liked me— the way my uncle cornered me and tried to touch me where he shouldn't— but how I got away. She knew that I got homesick and that I used to have a crush on my teacher but somehow I couldn't seem to tell her about praying.

Grandmother said it was "the devil" that kept me from telling people. But I never came close to sharing it and what I thought was that that made God sad. Right now, I wanted to tell Sally so much. "How do I tell her?" I prayed. "I think it would make her feel better."

I prayed at night before I went to sleep and at meals, but what I'd never told Sally before was that one of the main things I did on my rock was to talk with God.

But right then, I think God put in my mind the scene of the first time I could remember that I had prayed. And a cat was there. It would be great to share with Sally right now.

"You want to hear a story about Alice Hobbs and me?"

"Sure." Sally sat up and stretched. I could always count on her to like my stories, just like I liked hers.

"Well you know how Alice Hobbs and I waited together for the school bus every morning?"

"Sure."

"This happened when I was very young. Mother and Daddy paid tuition for me so that I could start to school when I was five years old. It was Friday of my first week and I'd had a hard time because every other day that week, I'd lost my lunch money. Monday, the teacher sent me to eat with the kids who got 'free lunch' because they couldn't afford to pay. I was truthful and told Mother. On Tuesday—I couldn't find it again and one of my friends shared her lunch that she'd brought from home. Mother was pretty mad. Wednesday I got there with my money but Thursday it had dropped out of my pocket somewhere. I was too ashamed to tell anyone and I pretended I wasn't hungry. Mother figured it out anyhow when I came home from school and ate a whole plateful of her oatmeal cookies." Sally laughed and that helped me go on telling the story.

"Where do you think things go when they die?"

"That Friday morning, Mother tied my lunch money in the corner of my handkerchief. She was sure that would do the trick, and she told me it had better work! Alice and I were waiting for the second bus. See, our school didn't have enough busses so they had to make two trips on some of the routes. We were playing up on the golf-course—the part of it that goes up the hill on the other side of Highway 71." Sally nodded. "It was almost time for the bus to come and I reached into my pocket. My handkerchief was gone!

I was so shocked. I felt sick. I told Alice that Mother would be so upset with me that she that might even make me quit school. Alice started looking everywhere and it was getting later."

"Just don't tell her," she shouted.

"I was standing there thinking that it wouldn't be right not to tell her, when all of a sudden I remembered that Grandmother always told me if I was in trouble—to pray. So I said, 'Let's pray, Alice!' She looked at me kind of funny but when I folded my hands and bowed my head—she did too."

"Well—did God give you your lunch money?" Sally asked.

"I think so."

"What do you mean, you think so?"

"You'll never believe this, Sally. We opened our eyes and not far from us was a big yellow tomcat. He was batting something around as if it were a mouse. We went over to see, and—it was my handkerchief..."

"AND your lunch money." Sally completed my sentence.

"YES."

"So a cat taught you to pray."

"No, not really. My grandmother taught me to pray and my mother, and this morning I prayed that you wouldn't feel so bad and I prayed for Kitty Thirteen, too."

"Oh," was all that Sally said.

I waited and waited. She had her eyes closed.

Finally, she asked, "What else do you pray about?"

I couldn't think what to say. I'd told her this morning about my feelings about the party and all about the paper dolls. And I'd told her about the reasons I came to my rock. What else could I tell her?

Then I heard her say: "I pray sometimes about the mean people." Her voice was hard to hear because she had her head down on her arms.

She sat up and said something that didn't make sense to me. "I pray about people who are snooty to others because of what they are. Sometimes it hurts a lot."

I glanced at her. Her face surprised me. She looked almost as angry as when she had heard our kitty was run over. All I could think to do was to squeeze her hand. We sat for a while longer staring out at the hills.

You could hear the buzz of a mosquito near us and the "kaboom" of the rams far below. The sun got hotter and hotter and the birds stopped singing. I felt little trickles of perspiration on the back of my neck.

Sally stood up and shook her long hair as if to break the spell. "Let's go swi-mming my darling daughter!" she belted out.

"Ready!" I jumped up and started climbing down off the rock, knowing she'd tell me more when she was ready. I was glad I'd shared the lunch money story. I was happy she was my friend. Everything would be all right. In my heart I told Grandmother that she was right. When you are in trouble—pray and God will help you.

Dear Diary,

After swimming, we went out in the boats. My choice. It's fun and scary when you start out 'cause if you get too close to where the water goes under the dam, you might be sucked under with it. We spent about two hours exploring the other (far) end of the lake where there are all those little inlets. Sally was swinging her paddle around acting like she was a native. She hit a wasp's nest! We both got stung and had to paddle back in a hurry. Just as we got nearly to the boat dock, Sally stood up and "accidentally" fell in. (No one is supposed to swim in the lake but she was itchin' something awful.) Joe had come down to call us for dinner and when he saw her, he pulled off his shoes and swam in after her. She was mad—but don't you think he was kind of sweet to do that?

Connee

Chapter 13

Celebration

It was the last day that I would be staying with the Matofskys. Tomorrow I'd begin running the Plunge and working nights at the Pavilion dances. It was Sally's turn to choose our adventure and I knew she was up to something. She was so creative. Her friends in Tulsa get her in on planning the parties. Last fall, her mother even asked her to help her give a baby shower.

They planned it for the back yard where there were lots of yellow chrysanthemums blooming. Sally made big signs and had some of her buddies to help her act them out while she slid them down the clothesline. The signs said: Jill Is Born, Jill Takes First Step, Jill Goes To School and Jill Has First Date. Then: Jill Marries. Then Sally carried one that had written on it in big letters: TIME MARCHES ON (just like the newsreel before the picture show.) She walked down to the end of the clothesline and there was a baby basket full of presents for Jill—the "mother to be."

Our gang of friends had parties too, in the wintertime. We used the Fun Encyclopedia for our ideas. They were good, but if Sally lived here, we'd have even better ones.

Sure enough—here she came with a big sign done in pastels saying:

SCRAWNY? CORNY? NO!
CONNEE!
or
CONSTANCE VIRGINIA MAY!
No matter what you are called:
This is Your Day.
To Celebrate
WE LOVE YOU
Mr. Matofsky, Mrs. M,
Joe and Hilda

Next we had one of Hilda's best breakfasts with bacon and eggs, and pancakes, orange juice and strawberry preserves. I was careful not to eat too much and Joe was careful not to say anything about spilling. Not one time. After breakfast he played cards with us and then they told me they were taking me for lunch to the Horseshoe Café. It was my favorite place in Bentonville. I could hardly believe it. I felt like a queen.

The next good thing that happened was that I saw two of my friends, Susie and JoAnn Firestone drinking a Coke. Sally and I went over and said "Hi." Then, when we sat down, Mr. Matofsky told us that we could each have the seventy-five cent plate lunch. That's the biggest and best. I'd had the fifty cent one, but never the other. For dessert I had coconut cream pie, another thing I really loved.

"Now comes the best part. Daddy has a great surprise. Let's run get in the car first," Sally said—pulling me out the door. We drove and drove what seemed like hours. Mr. Matofsky stopped for gas and actually bought us all a Coca-Cola after that big dinner. Then we came to a sort of farm. Sally was so excited she almost popped. "This is it! This is it! We're here," she squealed.

It was a pet farm. Inside were the most beautiful kittens and cats I'd ever seen. Mr. Matofsky had discovered it and now he wanted each of us to have a new kitten. "I know it won't take the place of your little Kitty Thirteen," he said in his kind voice, "but I want each of you to choose one that you like."

Joe went off to look at the dogs and Mrs. M came over smiling and said, "Sally, you choose from this pen."

She pointed out another pen for me. I chose a dear Persian with long gray and brown hair and a sweet face. She was chasing her tail and I knew her name would be "Frisky." Sally picked a kitty the color of deep blue, with even longer hair than mine. She named her "Beauty" and told me on the way home she had named it after me.

It was our last night to sleep together and the kitties curled up together in their little bed as if they knew it would be their last night together, too.

"I know it won't take the place of your little Kitty Thirteen…"

Dear Diary,

Sally will always be my best friend. I love her with all my heart. I'll miss being up here. Today was so nice that I hate the way I'm feeling. As we were leaving the Pet Farm, I heard Mrs. M tell the man to be sure to send the papers on Sally's cat. She appreciated the nice "mixed breed" he sold her for me. Now isn't this silly? I love Frisky already. I love her even better than Beauty. Why do I feel cheated about my special day? I'll bet Mr. Matofsky didn't know. I'm sure Sally didn't. Oh, I wish I didn't feel this way. I have to pray. Good night, Dear Diary. Confused.

Chapter 14

Back to Work

I opened my eyes and saw my old pump organ across the room from my bed, and Mother's winter coat hanging in a bag outside my closet door. The blue Dutch Boy quilt that Grandmother had made was on the foot of my bed. Home. Of course, it wasn't wintertime with bacon and coffee and hot biscuit smells in the kitchen, but this was my room and my bed and my house. I was home.

The note on my pillow just said: "Dear Connee—COME—I love you. Mother."

I yanked on my yellow "look-alike" shorts, clean socks and saddle oxfords and ran all the way to the Pavilion. I'd worked at the swimming pool on my first day back but today it was closed for cleaning, so I was to help at the fountain. Mother was back in the restaurant talking to the waitresses and by the time we'd hugged there were customers to be waited on out front.

All morning I sold candy bars and concocted cherry Cokes, Dr. Peppers and root beers by pushing the knobs that had different kinds of syrup and filling them with carbonated water from the fountain. One boy wanted a suicide. That's when you put every single flavor in, even chocolate.

Some ordered sodas, too. I'm really proud of how I made sodas. First you used an ice tea spoon to mash up some ice cream and chocolate or cherry syrup in the bottom of a tall glass. Then you pushed the carbonated water spigot backward and it came out in such a hard stream that it mixed the concoction. Next, you added a large scoop of vanilla ice cream and then turned the spigot back again so that the strong force of the carbonated water hit it making foam all the way to the top. Just before you served it—you'd plop another scoop of ice cream in and it sank down into the foam. Mouth watering!

In between customers, I tanked up on a milk shake and ate most of a hamburger someone had ordered but then didn't take. There was a long lull at about one thirty. Everyone went on a break, so I dropped down in a chair to rest. I put my head down "just for a minute" and I guess I fell asleep. Someone blew on my hair and I jerked awake. It was Sally with Jiggs and Lady. All three of them paraded around me. She was laughing and Lady was barking and Jiggs danced around on his hind legs bouncing his front paws on my bare arms. I petted him and laughed, too. I was so glad to see them.

No one came for a long time so we got to use my slugs to play the pinball machine and the nickelodeon. When we got tired, we played at the penny pitch. That was a big square of shiny wood with painted numbers on it and a rail all the way around that you could lean on and throw down pennies. If you landed on a number—like a seven—and not on the black line drawn around it, you'd won yourself seven pennies.

I put on the hat with the green shade that they wore at night to keep the light from shining in their eyes and raked Sally's pennies into a trough that ran all around the edge. She kept saying "oops" when she landed on the lines. She wanted to keep on playing even when she'd lost all of her pennies. The customers at night were that way too. They hated to give up. "Okay, your turn," she told me as she reached for the long handle of the rake and took the green shade off my head. I tied the green canvas apron around her, too. It had pockets to hold the money so that you could make change.

Some guys from the University of Arkansas came up and wanted to pitch pennies, so we had to quit. They weren't too happy about not letting them, but I talked them into one of my famous thick milkshakes. I would never spin 'em too long, so they were real thick, and they had tiny pieces of ice cream that tasted heavenly going down. While they drank them, I opened the glass showcase for Sally to take a sniff. Snickers and Milky Ways and Powerhouses mixed with Juicy Fruit gum. Nothing smelled better. She loved the cigar case, too. Said it reminded her of her daddy. "Oh, that reminds me," she said, fishing in her pocket for some gum wrappers. "Here's some more tin-foil for W. T."

"He left it for me," I told her as I ran back in the kitchen to get the big silver ball he'd worked on ever since the war began. He'd peeled the silver liner off the inner part of a million gum wrappers and wadded and pressed them together. Every one he knew saved them for him and sometimes he went through trashcans to look for more. He told me that when I got it as big as my head, I could turn it in for the "War Effort."

"Don't forget—you said we'd dig for money," Sally reminded me. I'd told her stories about how W. T. and I found some around the Pavilion where it had burned several years ago.

I was afraid the ground was too hard and what if we didn't find any? So, I asked her if she wanted to use the Shooting Gallery instead. I wasn't sure if I should turn it on, but I so wanted Sally to have fun. She was a whiz at knocking down the metal rabbits and squirrels with a pellet gun as they came around on the track.

Uneasy that Mother would come back, I said "Sally, I've got to get this change counted in a hurry. Do you know how?" Curious, she flipped off the switch and put away the gun.

"This is something Daddy taught me," I told her in a proud voice, as I spread out a bunch of coins on the counter. "Use your pointer and middle finger and pull off the dimes or nickels—just so they are the same kind— pull 'em off the counter into your other hand. Then make a loose fist and shake the money until it'll go into a stack. It's easy, try it."

Anything Sally did, she kept at it until she had it perfect. She learned fast and had stacks of quarters and dimes and nickels each adding up to a dollar or fifty cents. "It makes it easy to count change in stacks, doesn't it?" I asked her, putting the coins in the cash register.

"Absolutely. I'm going to show Daddy how. The men in his company might just need to know this." One thing about Sally, she always made you feel like everything you did was important.

I couldn't think of anything else to offer her to do so I asked her if she wanted one of my favorite drinks. Of course she did. I shaved a glass full of ice off the block then poured milk over it and stirred in Hershey's chocolate. "Try it."

She took a big sip and said, "Ummm, good."

"It's called a Jew Milk."

Sally spewed the drink all over the counter.

I grabbed the glass and looked in it. "What's the matter? I'm sorry, was the milk sour or something?"

Sally spun off the stool and went over and sat at the ice cream tables.

Bewildered, I came out and sat with her. The corners of her mouth were down and even her golden tanned face looked pale. "Why do you call it that?" she demanded.

"Gee, I don't know. I never thought why. It's just what we've always called it. I'm so sorry. What do you care?"

"Okay, Connee, I'm going to tell you what I meant about mean people when we were up on your rock the other day. Just because my family is Jewish there are those that don't want us around."

"But I thought you went to the Methodist church."

"We do. But we are Jews, even if we don't go to a Temple. Not many people know it, but once my daddy was going to join a country club and they told him he wasn't welcome. He found another one that didn't know and they were very happy to take him right in. Really, it bothers my mother more than him. She won't talk with me about it though, except to tell me to 'keep still about it'."

"That's crazy. You are just people."

"It's even happened to me, Connee. If it hadn't been for my friend, Mary Grace, I would never have gotten into our club at school."

"How did she help you?"

"Someone heard a rumor that I was not 'okay.' Mary Grace knew I was Jewish but she loved me and wanted me in the club. She said, 'Oh, no. Sally is Russian!' The ninnys. They didn't go on with their investigation. Yes, I am Russian. A Russian-Jew. I got to join and even later became president. They never knew." She said this with an impish grin that made me feel better.

"I always felt a little bit uneasy," she went on, the scowl coming back on her face. "I was scared they'd find out—but at the same time—I wanted to tell them to see if they'd still like me. We were all such good friends—how could it have made any difference? But I never did."

For once, I couldn't think of a thing to say. It was all so crazy. I'd never heard of anything like that before. I just sat there.

It was so like Sally to make me at ease. "C'mon, mah friends," she mimicked President Roosevelt. "I love you, Eleanor loves you, and our dog Fala loves you. How about telling us something funny."

"Well—someone pushed the plug out of the peep hole in the Ladies Restroom. Aren't you glad we've been changin' our suits at your cottage?"

"I wonder if they peeped when Freda was dressing?"

Freda was a high school girl who we accidentally splashed when we were playing tag at the pool. She would get in the water but she never wanted her hair to get wet. We told her we were sorry but she was so catty to us that the next day, when we swam near her, we splashed a little, "accidentally on purpose." She was so mad that she said she was going to report us to Mr. May. We just died laughing over that.

Just imagining her dressing and not knowing someone was watching, we both began to laugh again. Every time we'd stop, one of us would start again. We had the "Selby Giggles."

Selby Giggles were when you start laughing and couldn't stop. My grandmother was named Selby. She was a very serious person. That's why it was so funny when she got tickled and laughed 'til she cried. All of my cousins and aunts and uncles called it the "Selby Giggles" including some of my friends at school.

Then Sally said, "I know—if no one else comes, tell me the secret of the disappearing act that the orchestra boys do in their floorshow. Julia Ann was talking about it at the party."

"Well, I'll give you a hint. With W. T. gone, they won't be able to do it any more!"

"He's part of it? Tell me." She sat on a stool at the fountain and began twirling it back and forth.

"Okay, promise you'll never tell anyone though."

"NEVAH"—Boy Scouts honor."

"You aren't a Boy Scout, silly."

"Yeah, but I got Boy Scouts' honor."

"Okey dokey, now here's the scoop," I said in a low voice.

"See, some nights they do this show during intermission. They put down their instruments and pretend they're a circus. Everyone digs out clown masks and silly hats and then 'Bubbalou'—the real tiny guy that plays clarinet—acts like he's a weight lifter. But the dumbbells aren't heavy. I've lifted them and they're light as broomsticks, even though they look like they weigh a whole lot. He tries and tries and tries and finally lifts the dumbbells up—but then he collapses.

Anyway, three of the orchestra boys rush over toward him with a stretcher, making lots of noise. While you're watching that, another one sneaks over and opens a trap door. Bubblalou jumps through it and W. T. catches him down below in the men's bathroom. And the men with the stretcher and all the others in the orchestra yell—'Where'd he go? He's disappeared!'"

84

"Mikedosh, let's go see it." She jumped up and ran toward the back of the Pavilion. I ran after her yelling that we'd have to see it fast before customers came.

"All it is, is a trap door in the ceiling—see?"

We looked up and Sally stroked her chin like Sherlock Holmes. "Hmmmm, You're right. Nothing but a trick trap."

We ran back around to the front and sure enough, a couple of kids were sitting at the fountain waiting for an ice cream cone.

After I'd served them double dips, Sally said, "'Gotta go. Can I take Jiggs? Daddy hoped he'd stay with us the rest of the summer."

"Oh, I can't do that. It wouldn't be right. But I'll let him out early so he can go walkin' with Lady. I have to open the pool by nine."

"And you know I'll be there. Do you start waiting tables here tonight?"

"Yes, I'll be sleepy tomorrow won't I? But I love the music. It's Mel Crismon's Orchestra. Wanna hang around 'till Mother comes back and go up with me to their practice? They might get into a jam session."

"Better not. Maybe next time. Is it fun?"

"Yes! Remember how I told you about this same orchestra that came when I was a little girl? Mother hadn't taken me to Grandmother's yet so I came over here a lot. Marilyn Malone was the singer. She'd let me sit on her lap while they all played whatever they wanted and took turns at solos and played all around the tune."

"How old were you?"

"Oh, only four or five, I guess. Marilyn would kiss my cheek and say how much she wanted a little girl like me someday."

"Did she ever have one?"

"I don't know. Maybe I'll ask Mel when there's a chance. I've got to be sure he remembers me."

"Are you crazy, Connee May? No one would ever forget you."

Sally made me feel beautiful. But she was the beautiful one. Her friend Mary Grace, from Tulsa said they thought she was the most beautiful girl in school. All my friends said she was a glamour girl if there ever was one.

She left then. I told her this was an "Arkansas Good-bye." You said you were leaving and then you came back and talked awhile then you had to say goodbye again. We always hugged. She was like a sister. I would never, never want anyone to snub her. It made me hurt to think about it.

"I told her this was an "Arkansas Good-bye."

Then, for the first time, it sank in that I was not going to be staying with her for the rest of the summer. She'd be in Bella Vista, but I'd be working. It wouldn't be the same. I felt a pang of homesickness. But then some more customers came.

Chapter 15

Island Scare

We had been so busy all day. Fourth of July brought one of the biggest crowds to the pool and people bought a million things to eat and drink at the Pavilion then stayed for the big fireworks display. Like every year, Daddy went out early in the morning to the island in the lake and spent hours getting the crew to build frames and help him place all of the fireworks according to the diagram he'd made. Then when it got to be "dark-thirty," he went out alone. It was amazing how he could set off each one in the right order.

My daddy could figure out just about anything. He was great at arithmetic. When there was a problem, he would sit down with a pencil and a Big Five tablet and concentrate hard. I knew not to talk until he was finished.

We used to have awful floods in the spring before he had the idea of the floodgates on the two bridges by the spillway. I never told him and Mother, but I really loved the floods. I'd wake up in the morning and hear a roar and think—flood! No way to get across the spillway to catch the school bus. Yea!

For Daddy, it was no fun though to get the mud cleaned out of the Pavilion and the roads repaired. He'd have a crew cleaning up the minute the water went down. Daddy worked from daylight until dark, seven days a week in order to get the resort ready to open June 1st. It flooded year after year and he had to do something. So he made the floodgates and they controlled the lake each time Sugar Creek rose after too much rain. Daddy was so smart.

That's why what happened surprised everyone so much. When the first explosion of fireworks went off, there were beautiful blue stars showering across the sky. The crowds all around the lake were sitting on blankets and cars and eating all kinds of junk while they "ooood" and "ahhhd" over the show. Mother had let all the waitresses go out on Moonlight Gardens to watch. (That was a floating dance floor that you could walk out on from the Pavilion. It went way out over the lake and had little tables all around with umbrellas thatched with dried cattail leaves.) Right now there weren't many customers and we could take turns waiting on them.

Mother and I were both busy when it happened. There were deafening explosions and the sky lit up with silver and gold stars and balls of roman candles and American flags and whizzing, whirring sounds followed by more explosions.

All the fireworks had gone off at the same time!

There were cheers and screams and applause and laughter—then someone yelled: "Oh God, what about Whitey?" People started yelling, "Whitey"… "Mr. May"… "Are you all right?" Mother and I ran out as far as we could on Moonlight Gardens. The fireworks kept exploding.

Mother put her arm around me and we strained our eyes to see. I could feel her heart pounding. Then we heard the cheers. Someone had spotted my daddy. He was swimming through the lake to safety.

"I should have known he'd do something like that," I chattered, loosening my tight grip on Mother's arm. "Dr. Compton came out here from Bentonville the other day and he told me that before I was born, Daddy used to dive into the lake off the 30-foot diving board. And remember when the pigs were caught in the barbed wire fence that spring during the flood? Remember how he swam down and turned them loose so they could get to higher ground?" I just couldn't stop talking and inside I felt shivery and happy.

"Yes, that's your daddy." She smiled, looking relieved, then she changed to her "busy" voice to say, "C'mon girls, there'll be a big crowd to wait on now."

She was right. People poured in. Our very first customers were Sally and Mrs. M and Joe. They congratulated Mother and Joe shook her hand. He told Mother the crowd had lifted Daddy out of the water and held him up and cheered and clapped. It was great to see them. Sally pulled me to one side and told me that she had been rooting for my daddy. She hugged me so tight. Then the rush was on and I never knew when they left.

For once, Mother and I closed the place down. Uncle C. A. came in and stayed with us through the dance. He told us that he had gone out to

"People started yelling, 'Whitey'…'Mr. May'…'Are you all right?'"

the crowd around Daddy and sent him home to rest. But when we dragged in after midnight, Daddy was still sitting up. He had his diagram laid out on the kitchen table and had figured out where the mistake was that made the fireworks blow each other up. He looked more tired than we did. I don't think he liked to make mistakes.

Chapter 16

Money Dive

"Don't you ever get tired of working and not playing?" Sally asked.

She and I were sitting in the little office where I sold tickets and checked season passes. I wasn't supposed to have anyone with me but she had to wait thirty minutes after she ate before she went swimming. I just couldn't tell her to sit outside. Mother and Daddy had explained to me that it didn't look business-like to have kids around; besides I might get distracted and make the wrong change. But it was really tough when my friends came out from Bentonville or one of the cottage owners' kids wanted to visit with me. And Sally was like family.

She wanted to count out the change like I'd showed her. We got all the dimes, nickels, pennies, and quarters in the right bins in the cash register and meanwhile I'd thought of a way to work out the problem about having someone with me in the ticket office. It's really a mess when you want to do what's right and you also don't want to hurt your friend's feelings.

So, I took her out to check things around the pool. Using the net with the long pole, we seined out the bugs that had fallen in during the night along with a couple of candy wrappers and a paper cup. Somehow, one of the lifesaver rings had fallen off its hook on the wall. I was supposed to throw one to anyone who looked like they are drowning. I hadn't had life-saving training, but I'd read that you might try to save someone by swimming out to him and if he panicked, he could claw you and climb up on top of you because he was trying to get out of the water. I sure didn't want to be the one that drowned.

The trouble was trying to figure out when someone was just teasing. I knew that Joe was a good swimmer, but once he was floundering around in the deep end and yelling, "help." I watched him a little bit and he seemed frantic. The minute I threw the lifesaver into the air, I could have killed him. He started laughing and laughing and calling me "the hero." He just kept on teasing me and saying, "Thanks for the life-preserver, I'll throw it back and you can wear it for a necklace, because you ARE a hero!" OH, I could have throttled him.

All this had made me forget Sally's question but she never forgets. "So—tell me, 'working wonder,' don't you ever get tired and want to play?"

"I do play," I protested. "Whenever the rush is over, I run, jump in, and swim. Besides," I hurried on so she couldn't dispute me, "I really do like to work. It's fun. Daddy, Mother, W. T., and I all are proud of working. You said yourself I was lucky to get to do all the things I do." Sally agreed with that, gave me a smile, and pulled on her white bathing cap, then fastened the strap under her chin. I didn't know that before the day was over, I'd think about this conversation. A lot.

I'd forgotten that it was "Money Dive" day. Almost twice as many kids came to swim. A big carload of my friends from Bentonville came first. It was great to see everybody and right after that, Julia Ann Paisley and a lot of the resort kids showed up. There were new persons I'd never seen, too, probably renting cottages for a couple of weeks. There was a group from Fayetteville, too.

Then came Uncle C. A. He wore white pants with a sharp crease, a white shirt, and a Panama hat. While the kids cheered, he waved and grinned and saluted.

Once a month he came with two huge sacks of coins to throw into the pool. Boy did everyone scramble to grab some as they sank to the bottom. My job was to get the ones who swam well to stay in the deep end. The little kids and non-swimmers were supposed to get first turn at the money he threw in the shallow end. Usually it worked but today there were a lot that didn't know the rules. I kept sending big kids back to the deep end. Uncle C. A. glowered at me with disgust, then turned his smile towards "the public."

Finally, with the help of Sally and some of my other friends, I got them all sorted out—the good swimmers down on the side of the deep end and the others ready to get in where the water was only one or two feet deep. Uncle C. A. used a megaphone and asked them "Are You Ready?" in a dramatic voice. Of course they yelled "YES" at the top of their lungs.

Then they screamed and laughed when he acted like he was throwing a handful of money in, but stopped in mid-air.

I saw my Bentonville friends holding hands-ready to jump in together. I stood there feeling left out. It wasn't any fun to be one of the workers right then. Then, at that moment, everyone jumped into the pool, squealing and pushing and diving to grab the coins.

Uncle C. A. never realized how hard it was to make this event happen right. Lots of times he told other people I was a good worker. But sometimes he acted like I wasn't. Like today. He walked off without saying anything or even looking at me, and I'd wanted to please him so much. He could always get me to do extra jobs when he bragged on me.

Once he saw me making some signs and he said I might be an artist some day because I had real talent. I knew Daddy liked to be around him, too. Sometimes he was funny. One time he and Little C. A. (that's what Mother and Daddy called his son) came over to our house to have lunch. He loved Mother's cooking. That day, she had a cake right out of the oven. It was sitting on the table to cool so that she could ice it. Uncle C. A. asked Daddy to slice him a piece. Then they sliced one for Little C. A. Daddy ate a slice and Uncle C. A. said, "I think you cut that a little uneven, Whitey." They each had another piece and Uncle C. A. said he still thought it looked uneven. They got tickled and kept cutting and ate the whole thing! Mother came in to finish lunch and couldn't find her cake. When they looked sheepish, she realized what had happened and everyone had a good laugh.

It would have been great if he had always been that way, but just when you thought he approved of what you were doing, he'd make you feel so little. One time, for instance, he asked me what I thought of a high school girl he wanted to hire at the Sunset Hotel. I was honest and told him that she ran around with a bunch that drank and smoked. He said, "I didn't ask you about her personal life. That's none of your business. I wanted to know if you thought she would work hard." My face got red as fire. I was so ashamed.

I stood there remembering that day and then I thought of Sally's question, again. Didn't I get tired of working when everyone else was playing? Of course I wasn't allowed to go under water and hunt for money. I was working there. I was different. Suddenly everything didn't seem so clear after all. I turned to go to the ticket room. Pretty soon someone would want his basket with clothes and a towel.

94

"Suddenly everything didn't seem so clear after all."

Dear Diary,

Tonight was awful—awful! I was serving the big round table close to the front and had a tray with a lot of Cokes on it. Everyone was talkin' loud over the band and I forgot and took the bottles off that were closest to me. OH, NO! You know what that means. The outer edge was heavier and tipped over—right on a woman with a white dress. She jumped up and balled me out and kept sayin' MY DRESS IS RUINED! Everyone around us was looking. I was so ashamed. She told me I was a stupid girl. Oh, how could I have spilled? She just kept on and kept on. Finally, one of the men told her to stop—that he'd have it cleaned. He stood up and put his arm around me and said not to let her bother me. ARE YOU KIDDING? Oh, how can I be so dumb? I'll never get over this!

Chapter 17

Only One Dance

Dear Diary,

It's already August and I haven't written a word. I am so sleepy and tired when I get home at night after working and I hate to take you over to the pool. Someone might read what I wrote again. I'm sorry you've been hidden away in my dark closet. OOOO, were you scared? Last night was the Emancipation Dance. Emancipation Day is in June to celebrate when the slaves were freed. (It's called Junteenth) But in June, Uncle C. A. has the colored people working too hard as waiters at the hotel. So he holds this dance for them when the season is almost over. Oh, they are good dancers. They can jitterbug real fast! They shake their shoulders and the women can go almost down to the floor backward while still dancing. I love seeing their shimmery dresses with lots of gold and red and black. All us spectators sit around the edge of the roped off dance floor. Last night there was the biggest crowd ever. Lots of people couldn't get a seat and had to stand up to watch. Uncle C. A. used to let everyone come free, but now it's twenty-five cents for every person. Even me. I don't know where all the colored people come from! There aren't any who live around here. I wonder how they feel with all of us gawking at them? They don't ever look at us. Maybe they like it, like putting on a show. But why do they only get to come to the dance once a year? G'nite

"They can jitterbug real fast!"

Chapter 18

Swimmin' Nude

Yesterday was the last day of the season—Labor Day. The pool was closed to everyone but still not drained, so Mother and Daddy went for a swim. Yesterday a million people swam for the last time. Today, everything felt quiet and empty. Sally and her family and a visitor went up to Eureka Springs. Almost all the cottage owners packed up and left early this morning when the men came back from the city to get their families. Their cars were loaded down with people and boxes and pets. Some of the fathers couldn't come so they sent their chauffeurs.

I thought tomorrow I'd hike around to the cottages to see if any cats were left without a home. Always before I had looked forward to the nine months when we had Bella Vista almost to ourselves. Cottages would be boarded up and there would be hardly any traffic and we'd have time to be at home together. But somehow the end came too fast this year. With W.T. way down in Texas, and the Pavilion and the Sunset Hotel closed and Sally not here, I didn't know exactly what I wanted to do. I wandered from room to room, listened to "Little Orphan Annie" and "I Love A Mystery" on the radio, played with Frisky, and then went out on the porch and sat in the swing. By then it was getting dark and the moon was coming up. In the distance, I heard a splash and some laughter. That's when I had a great idea. At least I thought it was great. I decided to go swim with Mother and Daddy.

I pulled on my bathing suit—not easy since I'd left it wadded in a towel from yesterday and it was still cold and clammy. Its straps were wet too and it took several times to fasten the criss-cross at the back.

The moon was so full it seemed to have spilled over and covered me and all of Bella Vista with its light. Tree frogs were singin' their hearts out and the air smelled a little like rain. Or September. Mother always said September smelled different and that she had never gone through that month without missing going to school. That seemed so strange since she was so old. She was 37 in April.

I was barefoot and didn't want to step on a snake so I ran all the way around by the road instead of taking a short cut across the grass. The front gate was locked. I ran around to the fence and stood there catching my breath, ready to yell at them to let me in.

What I saw shocked me as much as if that fence had been hooked up to electricity. There were Mother and Daddy, plain as day in the full moonlight as they swam side-by-side out to the Top. They kissed and then climbed up out of the water. Mother was laughing and Daddy flicked water on her and was laughing, too. They didn't know that anyone was seeing them. They didn't know that anyone was in *miles* of seeing them. AND THEY WERE COMPLETELY NAKED!

I ran through the grass all the way back home to my bedroom— slammed the door and fell across my bed. I never felt so ashamed and embarrassed in my life. How could they? It was DISGUSTING! I drank hot Ovaltine and read and read but I couldn't get it out of my mind! When they came home, I faked being asleep.

Mother always taught me it wasn't right to eavesdrop. Tonight though, I cracked my door a tiny bit and listened. They were sitting close to each other on the couch. Thank heavens they had their clothes on! Mother told Daddy how glad she was the resort was closed. She kissed him on the cheek and told him it was special to see him have this little celebration since he'd worked so hard. He told her she deserved a reward for working so hard and kissed her cheek, too. They got up and turned off the light and went in their bedroom. I heard her say, "Same time again next year?" and he told her it was a date she could count on.

"They didn't know anyone was in *miles* of seeing them."

Dear Diary,

   Well, maybe my parents are nice after all. I guess I'm glad that they're romantic. I just wish it hadn't been MY parents swimming nude. I'll bet they would have felt sorry if I had stepped on a snake. I told Jiggs and Frisky. I had to tell someone. Now, good night to you. Sleep tight. Don't let the bedbugs bite.

   P. S. I'M SO MAD!!!!!

Chapter 19

The Last Ride

The Matofsky's came back and brought their visitor, Amelia Faye Dorman with them. All summer I'd looked forward to taking Sally on the day the stable boys rode the saddle horses back to their winter pasture. She had never been here late enough in the season before. It was all arranged but now everything was ruined. Sally said she couldn't go with me if we didn't take Amelia Faye along. I wanted so much for it to be just for Sally and me—our last adventure of the summer.

Year before last, her friend Mary Grace had visited for a week from Tulsa. She was lots of fun. She came to the pool with Sally and we played cards and climbed hills. But Amelia Faye was a stick in the mud. They came over to see me yesterday and I thought she was whiney as a baby. She'd be right in the middle today. I wanted it to be just for Sally and ME!

Everyone was saddling up when we got to the stables. I felt so ashamed of my attitude toward Amelia Faye that I offered her my horse, Tony. I knew Sal would want her horse, Snip and I was determined to be nice. Sally gave me a funny look but just shrugged her shoulders like she was saying "Oh, Connee—you don't have to do that." One of the guys brought Tony over and Amelia Faye tried to climb up on the wrong side. That was when we knew she'd exaggerated about how much she'd ridden horses. She sure looked like she could, though—a sophisticate with real jodhpurs and a silky gray shirt. She'd pulled her long blonde hair back into one braid and wore a black-billed cap. Tony moved sideways and almost stepped on her foot. She gave a little scream. Then Sally told the guys they'd better give her Ol' Ribbon.

Ol' Ribbon! The slowest, pokiest, stubbornist horse in the bunch. Still, I couldn't help but feel wonderful when I slipped up on my dear, beautiful Tony's back. He and Snip started off together. They knew it was a day for Sal and me—riding together, like always.

It was more than four miles to the farm where the horses lived for the nine months that Bella Vista was closed. They always poked along at first, before they realized where they were going. It was fun to see how they got peppier and peppier the closer they got to green pastures and home.

Ol' Ribbon kept up with us pretty well for a while. The three of us rode together and took up the whole road. But as always, Ol' Ribbon got slower and slower. Sally told Amelia Faye to give her a little kick with her heels still in the stirrups. She did. Of course, Ol' Ribbon was used to people trying that. She was a saddle horse and she was old. She'd had a million riders and she could tell by the way they kicked her if they knew what they were doing. Amelia Faye not only did not know how to make her move, she didn't even know how to guide her with the reins. They were still wrapped around the saddle horn.

Sal looked at me and I looked at her. She took one of the reins and I took the other. There we were going down the road, leading Ol' Ribbon with Amelia Faye on her back. Sally looked embarrassed, so I started singing like we do on the school bus. "She'll Be Comin' 'Round The Mountain" was the song that got all the riders joining in. Sally was singing real loud, too.

Amelia Faye finally took the reins and we went on for a long time, but then Ol' Ribbon got ornery again. She saw some grass she wanted that was under the fence beside the road, so she pulled over there and ignored Amelia Faye while she nibbled away. Sally hollered at her and then rode over and snapped her rump real hard. Ol' Ribbon moved with us for a while but then began to edge over to the grass again. Amelia Faye yelled to us to help her catch up. We had both turned our horses around when something happened that was hard to believe.

A guy sped around the curve in his red pick-up truck. When he saw a big bunch of horses ahead—he turned his wheel sharply to the left, hit a big mud puddle in the road and bounced a couple of times, then ran right into Ol' Ribbon! She reared up and her side came down on that barbed wire fence that stretched over the grass she'd been eating.

Barbed wire has sharp points that stick out to keep cows in the pasture and strange horses like Ol'Ribbon out. Poor thing, her eyes looked wild when those barbs stabbed her.

Then—the unbelievable happened. Ol' Ribbon began to race. She rushed past us and the next bunch of horses, then galloped passed the lead horse and galloped out of sight. We were so scared. We screamed: "Amelia Faye, Amelia Faye, Amelia Faye!"

Everyone started yelling, "Stop—Stop you Ol' Ribbon"! The lead horse began racing after her. Then came the wildest part—*all* the horses ran away, too. We jerked on the reins. Everyone yelled louder. None of us could stop them. They ran until they were gasping and wheezing and choking. But just about the time I thought they were all going to die and I was too—they ran under the arch over the road that says: "HAPPY HORSE RANCH" and stopped. Short. We almost flew over their heads they stopped so fast. The others jumped off and began to walk them around, patting their shoulders and talking gentle to calm them down. So that's what we did too. I began to chatter to Sally.

"Mikedosh! That was wild. I guess they sort of stampeded like they do in the picture shows." We were both shaky and trembly with excitement.

"Or maybe they thought Ol' Ribbon and Amelia Faye were on the home stretch," laughed Sally. "Amelia Faye—oh no, Connee! Where is she?" We both ran among the horses trying to find her. We saw poor Ol' Ribbon standing alone, looking dazed. But no rider rubbed her down. Amelia Faye had disappeared!

We pushed through the rest of the sweaty horses and—there she was, sitting on the steps of the big porch looking like a wreck. Her braid had come loose and her damp, kinky hair stuck to the dirt on her face. Her beautiful gray silk blouse hung outside her jodhpurs and some of the buttons were missing. The guy who had ridden the lead horse had given her a glass of water and was standing there looking concerned. Sally ran and put her arms around her. Amelia Faye put her head on Sal's shoulder, not able to talk. Suddenly, all my bad feelings were gone. This was Sally's friend. She could have been killed. I came over and put my arms around both of them. We all three began to cry. I think I was crying partly because of me. I promised God I'd never be jealous again and I also told him how glad I was that we were all safe. Especially Amelia Faye.

"Everyone started yelling, 'Stop—Stop you Ol'Ribbon'!"

Ol' Ribbon wasn't hurt much after all. Daddy drove out to the farm to check up on her that very night. Amelia Faye was fine, too. She and Sally and the Matofskys all left a couple of days later. I would have been very lonesome except for what happened to us at home. It was so bad. It was not anything like the race with 'Ol Ribbon. It was awful. It hurt so much. It happened to Daddy. It happened to Mother and me too and it happened to W. T. even though he'd already gone to college.

Chapter 20

That Horrible Day

Breakfast was started. I could smell the bacon frying and hear mother rustling around in the kitchen. I hurried—pulling on my jeans, half brushing my hair. I could hardly wait to get in there where it would be cozy and warm. Mother looked up from rolling out the biscuit dough and smiled but there were none of her usual cheery greetings. She dipped each biscuit in melted grease, put them in the old black biscuit pan, and popped them in the hot oven. Then she wiped the same counter over and over and opened and closed the same cabinet door.

I started to set the table for four and remembered, no W. T. Maybe mother was missing him, or worried about him. That must be what was wrong. Right now he was far away in Texas, working at the bookstore. In just two weeks he'd start at the University. I filled the glasses with milk. Maybe he'd meet a girlfriend and they'd fall in love. Oh, how romantic— to go to college. I daydreamed about a tall, good-looking boy. He'd see me and say, "Oh, Connee, you are so beautiful." He'd be overwhelmed by my dreamy looks and he'd keep looking in my eyes. We'd walk off holding hands and…

Daddy came in. He sat down without looking at Mother or me. His mouth was clamped shut in a straight line and he squinted his eyes making them look dark. I'd seen that look before. He was mad. They'd had an argument. That was what was the matter with Mother.

"Gladys, isn't breakfast ready yet?" Anytime he called her Gladys instead of Sweetheart, I knew things were bad. Mother opened the oven door and peeked at the biscuit. She closed it and shrugged her shoulders.

Daddy jumped up, grabbed his milk bucket off the nail and said in a loud voice, "Damn it, I'll eat when I get back." I flinched. I hated it when he got mad. One time he was so angry that he'd jerked off the tablecloth. All the dishes crashed on the floor and broke in a million pieces. Oh, please, dear God, I prayed….

He went out, slamming the back door. I scooped up Frisky and called back to Mother that I would go with him. Outside, when I passed the kitchen window, Mother was wiping the cabinet again and crying.

My words tumbled out as we walked down to the stables—half sentences, excited phrases that went from one subject to another. I wanted so much to change his mood. Besides, it had been a whole summer since Daddy and I had talked much. "Honey, why don't you put that cat down instead of carrying her?" he asked.

Hadn't he been listening? I'd already said it was her first time and that she might not follow. She'd want to, after she'd watched the other cats waiting to drink milk. I stubbed along the dirt road, quiet now, my feelings hurt. There had been a lot more to tell, but he didn't seem interested.

To get my mind off that, I daydreamed about the cats and Daddy's milking. He sat on the little three-legged milk stool and squeezed one tit and then another making hard spurts of milk into the metal bucket. It made a tune with two notes: "pinng ping, pinng ping, pinng ping." As soon as he had a regular rhythm going he'd turn one of the spigots toward a cat then back again to the bucket. The cat leaped up and caught the white stream in its mouth in midair. Frisky would imitate them and learn how to do it in one visit. Cats are good at catching on.

Not me. Daddy had explained to me how to take hold just like I was shaking hands then squeeze down gently. Mother tried to help me by filling a rubber glove with water so that I could practice on the fingers hanging down. When I tried it on Bessie though, the drops of milk I got were pitiful. I was afraid I'd hurt her. I think Bessie was afraid too, and after three or four times, Daddy didn't offer to let me try any more. That was okay. He enjoyed having his cow again after one of the stable hands milked her all summer.

Today was not a day when Daddy enjoyed himself though. Several times he yelled at Bessie to stand still. Once, she flicked him in the face with her tail. A horsefly was bothering her but Daddy was still upset when she did that. He stood up, kicked one of the cats and picked up the pail to go, even though it wasn't full.

109

"The cat leaped up and caught the white stream in its mouth in midair."

On the way home I trotted by him. He walked so fast. Just as I turned to see if Frisky was following, I saw a strange look on his face. It was all white. It was white around his lips, too. All of a sudden, he grabbed his arm and at the same time turned loose of the bucket. I stared at the white milk puddling in the road, sinking down between the rocks and mixing with the dirt.

"My heart!" His face was red now and his eyes bulged. "Get Mother!" he stammered and sank down on his knees.

I shot forward. The rocks stabbed my bare feet but I ran and ran then leaped up our front stairs, yelling: "Mother, Mother! Mother!" She rushed out, wiping her hands on her dishtowel, took one look at me standing there alone, then jumped in the car and gunned out backward stripping the gears. I waited there, scared and shaking. I knew my daddy had had a heart attack.

Chapter 21

Doctors See Daddy

Mother put her arm around Daddy's waist to help him up the stairs. I ran down the steps and put my arm around him on the other side. "I guess it's good I'm tall for my age," I said in a bright voice. No one answered and I thought: what a stupid, stupid thing to say. As we went through the front door, Daddy's legs buckled under him and we had to pull him onto the bed.

He looked so helpless lying there. Smaller than himself. I wasn't used to my daddy lying down in the daytime. Mother leaned over him and put her cheek next to his and whispered, "Oh Whitey. Oh darling." Then she turned to me. "Quick," she said, "Go call Dr. Pickens."

I hurried in, and picked up the phone receiver. "Oh, dear heavenly Father, don't let anyone be talking on our party line," I prayed. The line was clear. I cranked the phone hard, four or five times, furiously impatient for Rosie, the phone operator to answer. She was hard of hearing and we had to talk loud. Today, she didn't have any trouble hearing my message though. "Rosie," I blasted out, "Tell Dr. Pickens to come to our house. And hurry! Daddy's had a heart attack!"

Rosie did well. Before she disconnected me, I heard her yell to someone else in the office, "Hold everything, Whitey May is in trouble!" No telling how many other persons she called after that because by the time Dr. Pickens drove up there were the Hobbs, the McCools, the Cunninghams, the Bolains and I don't know who all else, standing in the yard.

The Linebargers even brought another two doctors that were still staying on in the Linderman Cottage. All the doctors examined Daddy. Then they filed into the kitchen. Dr. Pickens asked me to make coffee. I took out cups and Bessie's thick cream and some sugar. Uncle C. A. set Mother's fresh pie on the table that she'd baked early that morning. They ate and drank and talked and talked. I heard parts of sentences: ...the high blood pressure…, strain on his heart…, so young…. I stood in the doorway chewing my fingernails as I watched them shake their heads. It must be very bad. Their voices sounded like bees humming. Maybe the humming was in my head. I wondered if this was what it felt like to faint. Finally, they asked me to go and get Mother.

"Mrs. May," one of the doctors Uncle C. A. had brought began talking, "It is our opinion…" Dr. Pickens interrupted. "Gladys, dear, Whitey's heart is very bad. He'll never be able to work again. I'm so sorry. We think it will just be a matter of time…" Mother gave a sob and then went back to Daddy.

Friends, who by now were packed into our tiny living room, began to tell each other how it wouldn't seem right without Whitey. "Why, he always does more work than all the rest of us put together," one of Daddy's crew said.

Others were speechless. I couldn't imagine Daddy not working. He always worked. People kept patting me on the shoulder and shaking their heads. The room got quiet and they began to file out, hats in hand. As they went by the open bedroom door, several of them said. "Hang in their Whitey. You'll be all right."

Dr. Pickens took my hand and we went in to Daddy and Mother. "Whitey," He said in a shaky voice, "It's pretty bad. I'm leaving you these pills to help you sleep. Don't get up. Don't do anything. I'll be out to see you tomorrow."

He left and there were just the three of us in there alone. Daddy looked at each of us and said something to me that was so sad. "Oh honey, do you realize I'll never be able to climb a Bella Vista hill again?" I kissed his cheek and went into my bedroom and shut the door. I couldn't wait to let down and cry and cry.

"I guess it's good I'm tall for my age."

Dear Diary,

Tonight, Mother told me that they were going to cut Daddy off without any salary. Right in the middle of the month! Mother said they wouldn't be taking their pleasure trip for at least two weeks. She sounded bitter! She lay down in my bed with me and I could tell she'd been crying because he eyes were so puffy. She told me that she just couldn't understand it, 'cause Daddy had worked so hard. She said there were so many, many times when he was too tired but had to keep on doing MORE. She thinks it will just kill Daddy when she tells him. She says he'll feel like he's lost a father. She cried some more and then said she's known all along that Daddy was being used—and that it proves it 'cause now that he can't do the dirty work—he's being thrown away. I've never heard Mother talk like that before. She didn't sound like herself. I don't know what to do—I know one thing, though! I'll NEVER CALL HIM UNCLE C. A. AGAIN!!!

Chapter 22

The Letter

Miss Connee May
Rt. 4
Bella Vista, Arkansas

Miss Roseanne Matofsky
39 Riverside Drive
Tulsa, Oklahoma

Dear Sally,

Aren't you surprised to hear from me? I'm typing this letter like our teacher taught us, because I have a lot to say. I wish you were here! I really do need to tell you what happened. Yesterday started okay. Daddy had been taking tickets up at the Cave for a week. See—Mother had asked (without Daddy knowing it) if there wasn't some way we could make some money. Daddy was supposed to get a tenth of any tickets he sold. He rested on our army cot and got a great tan. The trouble was that there were only five sightseers all week.

This morning he asked me if I wanted to go into Bentonville with him and Mother. He said he was NOT GOING TO LIE AROUND AND WAIT TO DIE. He said he was going to try to buy this small grocery and filling station in Bentonville, if the bank would loan him the money. We would move to town and I'd get to walk to school and then I could come home every afternoon and wait on customers while he rested. I was so excited. Can you imagine me living in Bentonville?

I told Daddy I'd give him all the tips I'd saved in my metal box. I think there are at least forty dollars. He stopped the car and looked around at me in the back seat. He said—"You would, wouldn't you?" I could tell that he was proud of me.

They had me wait in the car while they went into the Bank of Bentonville. My heart sang when they came out with big smiles. They got the loan and we could buy the store. Mother told me that they said, "Whitey May, we know your word is as good as gold. If you say you'll pay it back, you'll pay it back." Then they all shook hands on the deal. Mother was SO happy. Me too.

We went around to Banks Grocery and Mr. Banks gave me a big sack of candy just like he does when we pay our grocery bill every Saturday night, and it wasn't even Saturday. At home Jiggs danced around, so happy to see us and Mother cooked steak and eggs like it was Sunday night, but the steak wasn't left over bits from Sunday dinner. We each had a piece all our own.

I went to bed so happy, but in the middle of the night I heard this terrible sound. I got up and cracked my bedroom door and you'll never guess what it was. My daddy was crying! I've never, never heard him cry before, Sally. It was awful.

Mother had her arms around him and he kept saying he was afraid and what if he didn't make a go of it and we couldn't pay the money back. I never thought he could be afraid of ANYTHING. But, I never thought about him having a heart attack, either. I'm afraid, too. What is going to happen to us? What if he died? I wish you were here!!!!!

Love, your friend,

Connee

Chapter 23

The Call

I had never had a long distance call before. I thought Rosie the telephone operator, was kidding me. Also, lots of times, when I was talking to a friend, she'd be listening in and would give her opinion about something we'd said. I'd heard Daddy have to say to her, "Rosie, this is Whitey. May I please have the line to myself?" Then she'd bang down her receiver.

"Miss Connee May—long distance" is the way she said it. I was trying to think of something funny to say to kid her back when I heard this familiar voice.

"Hi, cheerful Constance" is the way she started. It felt good all over to hear Sally's voice acting silly. I smiled for the first time in several days. Then she told me that I hadn't been cheerful at all and she was calling to tell me why.

Now, she sounded serious. "I'll tell you what's the matter with you, Miss Connee May. Listen well because my Mother said I could only talk three minutes. Your trouble is that you need to go to your rock!"

"What?" I could hardly believe that she was saying this.

She thought the connection was bad and so she said it again. "Your rock, the one at the Big Spring. You know, Connee—that's where you said everything made sense. That's where you..." and she paused, "That's where you go to pray, isn't it?"

"Yes. Yes, Sally, you're right. I will. Thanks. Thank you so much. Thank you for calling." I couldn't think of another word to say.

I guess she couldn't either. We both were still and then she said, "Well, I gotta go. I love you."

"Me, too. Me too"—and then we both hung up.

"Your trouble is that you need to go to your rock!"

I don't know why her idea meant so much to me. Lots of other people had reminded me to pray for Daddy. Grandmother had—and my Sunday School teacher, Mrs. Bond, and our preacher, Brother Harold. But I hadn't been to My Rock. To have Sally be the one to think of it was like the piece that fits just right in a puzzle. It had been lying there all the time and I couldn't see it. Sally was a true friend and she knew what I needed even before I did. Maybe she was even praying, too.

I went over and lay down on the couch with my head on Daddy's pillow where he'd cried that night. A saying I'd heard went over and over in my mind. I felt like singing it so I made up a little tune: "God's in His heaven and all's right with the world!"

Chapter 24

Moving Day

Alice Hobb's daddy came with his truck to help us move. I had all my stuff packed and had cleaned all the music out of my pump organ so nothing would fall out when they lifted it. Jiggs looked worried and kept walking right where I needed to be. Three times I almost tripped over him.

Daddy looked great and didn't act worried at all. He seemed almost like his old self again. He stood on the front porch and directed Mother and me and the two boys from the Ventnor Farm who were helping. He'd been looking at the space in the truck and had it all figured out where each piece of furniture should go. Once in a while he whistled a line of some song but I couldn't figure out what it was. It didn't matter. The important thing was that he wasn't afraid.

Mother either. Neither of them would ever know that I heard them that night when Daddy cried. Only Sally knew. And God.

It seemed odd that I wasn't sad that we were leaving dear Bella Vista. True, I wouldn't be able to walk up to Big Spring or over to swim or ride the horses or work at the Pavilion. But right now I wasn't letting myself think of that. I was looking at my Daddy and Mother who were happy again. I was planning how much I would help at the new little store. I'd learn to pump gasoline and check the air in the tires. Maybe I'd check the oil. Mother would be working so I'd come home right after school every day and do my part. Daddy said he knew he could count on me. That was all I could think of right now. My daddy needed me.

It rained that first night I slept in my new room at the end of the little store. Mother and Daddy seemed far away in their apartment at the back. It was only five miles to Bella Vista, but I felt homesick, sort of like I felt those years in Shamrock, Oklahoma when I stayed with Grandmother.

There was an outside door in my room that opened to the backyard. Having it made me feel real grown-up until a big clap of thunder rattled my windowpane. Rain whirled in the wind and hit the window like buckets of water hurled at a fire. I ran over to pull down the shade. Lightning zigzagged through the sky and the trees bent back and forth in the swirling rain.

I pulled the covers up over my head. My heart beat faster. Then I heard scratching and barking and mewing. It was Frisky and Jiggs. They didn't like the lightning and thunder either. I hopped out, pushed the door open a little and they raced through and jumped on my bed before I could even dry them off. Under the covers together, they smelled like wet hair, but I didn't care. With them, I didn't miss Bella Vista quite so much. It felt like home had come with me. The storm quieted and I could imagine the rhythmical "'kaboom"of the rams at the Big Spring in the slow steady rain.

Next day the sun was shining and the postman walked right in to the front of the store and sat down to drink a coke. There wasn't much mail except for one incredible letter. It was addressed to "Miss Connee May" and was an invitation to go and visit the Matofskys. At last—I would see where Sally lived in Tulsa. I could hardly wait for Mother to get home. Surely she'd be so glad for me to get to go!

Chapter 25

Gusher Sundae

It felt strange to be with Sally in her house. She seemed older. Everyone did. All the furniture looked silky and plush like in magazines. Joe carried my suitcase and as we walked across the carpet it was so thick I felt like whispering. I caught a glimpse of the dining room as we walked by. In the center was a gleaming long table with dark polish. Over it hung a gigantic chandelier with hundreds of glass prisms dangling from it. The sun shone through it making rainbows on the walls and ceiling.

Mrs. M asked if I'd like some cookies and milk and I said, "Yes ma'm." Hilda served us in the breakfast room. She smiled but she didn't talk a lot like she did in Bella Vista.

Joe had set my suitcase down and disappeared. All of a sudden he opened the back door and Lady bounded in, jumped up on me and began licking my face. Mrs. M fussed at Joe but Sally and I couldn't help laughing. Good ol' Lady. At least *she* seemed the same.

That night I thought a lot after we turned the lights out. Sally had always wanted me to come and here I was. Daddy had caught me a ride part way with the guy who delivers mail and then managed to buy my bus fare for the rest of the way. I'd sat in the front and as I looked out of the windows on either side, the wind blew the red, orange, and golden leaves of the hardwoods. I imagined that they were people along a parade route waving their flags and cheering me on toward Tulsa.

Mother was so pleased that I could go that she had sewed late into the night to finish a new blue dress for me. The store where she worked let her off for the weekend so that she could help Daddy. Thinking about them made me have warm feelings. I wondered what they were doing right now.

Next, I thought about the dance Sally had mentioned. Would they do the same steps that we did? I'd danced as long as I could remember—in the winters Daddy gave me the key to the ballroom at the Pavilion. The jukebox was there and for nine months I played records free. I'd pretend I was dancing with one of the football boys and glide all over the big room. And in Bentonville we had great fun dancing, too. Some of the mothers had rented a store and called it the Junior Recreation Room. They chaperoned and made sandwiches just like it was a real U.S.O. that they have in cities for our servicemen. Red Cavness donated a jukebox. It had great records like "Moonlight Serenade," "String of Pearls," and "Stardust." I thought I was a pretty good dancer, but we all danced alike.

Maybe in Tulsa, I'd look like an Arkansas hick. Maybe I wouldn't know how to follow the boys here. Maybe they would laugh behind my back. I didn't want to be embarrassed. The worst thing would be if I would embarrass Sally. My mind kept going over and over it.

The next morning was much better. Hilda served Pear Honey and we all laughed remembering that contest Sal and I had had. Joe teased a little saying "Ah, come on, Scrawny, have just one more piece of toast."

After breakfast, we went on the city bus. I'd never been on one before and it was fun. We hopped on one and rode a while and then transferred onto another. The day was sunny and cool. Just right. I was amazed when Sally took me into lots of different department stores and we tried on millions of clothes but didn't buy anything. The clerks all knew her and kept urging us to try more. Several congratulated Sally, because her mother was the new PTA state president.

All the buildings were so tall and there were so many people. We went into a drugstore that was three times bigger than Crows or Applegates in Bentonville. As we sat down in a booth, a man in a suit came over and said hello. He wanted Sally to tell her father that he appreciated so much his help on their business deal. Oh my goodness. The Matofskys must be very important in this city.

At lunch, Sally took me to Woolworth's for lunch and acted silly like old times. She said her daddy picked her up at Camp Scott each year and always brought her straight here for a hamburger and milkshake because the food was horrid at camp.

Not until the bus ride home did the sinking feeling come back. That was when Sally asked me what I was wearing to the dance. Were there slippers to match the blue dress? I mumbled that I'd just brought my saddle oxfords. Mikedosh, I thought. Doesn't everyone wear saddle oxfords to a dance?

That night, my answer came in a way I wished it hadn't. Sally fell asleep early but I lay awake thinking what an exciting day we'd had. The Matofsky's bedroom was right next to Sally's, just like in Bella Vista. I could hear them talking but not until I heard my name did I tune it to what they were saying. "But, why can't Connee wear some of Sister's shoes, Mother?" (Mr. Matofsky always called Mrs. M "Mother.")

Mrs. M. sighed. "Oh, Sam her feet are just too big. They're a whole size larger than Sally's." My face flushed with shame. I strained to hear more but the voices got soft and then I heard Mr. Matofsky snoring.

Early the next morning I went down to the front porch and stood looking out at the tree-lined street and all the other big houses on Riverside Drive—all with views of the water. The steps were high and steep. I ran down them to take the morning paper from Lady's dripping jowls.

As I started back up, my heavy saddle oxfords stubbed on the stairs and I stumbled and fell. A wave of pain went through my ankle. I sat rubbing it—shocked and mortified when Mrs. M and Joe appeared. She had him carry me up to Sally's room. That embarrassed me so. I knew I was heavy. I was surprised that he didn't make fun of me for falling. Hilda rushed in with an ice pack. I lay there, my twisted ankle throbbing with pain and wished I could just disappear.

Sally hugged me and said, "I'm sorry." Then she stormed out—"Oh mikedosh—you won't be able to go to the dance tonight." My heart fluttered with relief and for a minute I was glad I'd hurt myself.

"No, I won't," I replied in a calm voice. "But you have to go and have a wonderful time. I don't want to spoil it for you." And of course, I really meant it. Now the dance wouldn't be spoiled. Now, Sally could brag about her beautiful blonde friend she had wanted to bring. Now I wouldn't make a fool of myself. I was saved.

The rest of the morning we played cards and drew crazy pictures and gabbed. Sally modeled her fuchsia dress and black patent leather slippers. She confessed how thrilled she was to go with Richard—one of the football boys who was in the grade above her. It was so easy to talk to her, just as it had always been. After all, we were best friends. But I did feel a little uneasy about not telling her that I wasn't disappointed that I couldn't go to the dance.

My foot felt a bit better so I hobbled down to lunch. Still, I made sure I didn't walk too well. I didn't want to take any chances that they'd think I had recuperated enough for the dance.

They didn't. Mrs. M smiled as if she had a secret and Joe was unusually quiet. Sally did most of the talking until her mother shushed her. "We have a surprise, Connee. You are going to a movie with Joe tonight."

"Oh—thank you," was all I could manage to say. Inside a little cloud of joy floated up into my chest.

Sally said it for me. "Oh great. At last, the two morons in my life are going to have a date."

She grabbed my hand and pulled me up the stairs not even thinking of my aching ankle. Inside she began tossing out jewelry, handkerchiefs, and makeup. She was in high gear.

"Try this and these—and you'll have to have a bubble bath and oh," she stopped short, "of course you'll have to wear hose."

I giggled with Sally. The idea of a real date. My first one. It was thrilling. I tried on blue earrings and looked into the mirror, and then Sally pronounced them perfect with my new blue dress. I tried it on and blessed Mother for it. It was long enough to hit my small waist just at the right point and the soft material fell into dreamy folds.

Later, I stood looking at my reflection again. I touched my first real corsage perched on my shoulder. They were gardenias. "They smell like my Heaven Scent perfume, don't they?" I asked Sally. She dabbed some on behind her ears and agreed.

I knew Mrs. M had fibbed to me when she said that Joe sent the corsage, but I didn't care. It was wonderful. Joe came and helped me down the stairs. Mrs. M probably told him to. But it was wonderful. My first date. Prince Charming. It would be wonderful. Wonderful, wonderful, wonderful! The word kept floating around me like a bubble and I didn't want it to break. We caught the bus to the movie. That's what they called it there instead of picture show.

Not until we got off the bus did I feel the hose slipping. Oh, I'd worn hose a few times before but always with a garter belt. Sally had provided garters. They were much too big. At first, I laughed to myself thinking that my feet might be large but at least my legs weren't bigger than hers. But, by the time we'd walked a block, I wasn't laughing. The silly hose were sliding down my legs. I stopped to look in a store window and pointed out something to Joe. Then I grabbed the garters and tried to twist them a little tighter. This helped for almost another block. "How much farther?" I asked, feeling desperate. In the four blocks left, I ducked into stores three times with the excuse that I wanted to see something. I just knew Joe would say something catty. He didn't. Finally we were in our seats and I could relax.

The show was funny and we laughed out loud and munched popcorn and I almost forgot my problem. But then the movie was over. I made the first block before stopping at an ice cream shop window to yank up my hose. They were almost to my ankles. Silently, I pleaded—*Oh, don't look at me.*

"We're going in," Joe said, his voice a little too loud. Thankfully, I slid into the delicate little ice cream parlor chair and reached down to pull up my crazy hose. I would never wear garters again as long as I lived. Now the corsage smelled too sweet. I felt sick.

"Excuse me," I blurted out and almost knocked over the little metal chair as I got up.

Alone in the rest room, I sat down on the lid of a potty. Suddenly an idea came to me. "Oh, you crazy girl." I told myself giddy with happiness. Why hadn't I thought of it before? I'd just take 'em off.

My fingers quickly rolled down those pesky hose right off my feet. My saddles felt a little odd with no socks but I tied the strings in bowknots with a flourish and stuffed the hose into my purse.

"I'm free, I'm free" I sang to myself and danced a couple of steps. I looked in the mirror and saw a beautiful girl with blue earrings, a silky blue dress and roses in her cheeks. I breathed in the white gardenias on my shoulder. They smelled heavenly again.

Joe must have noticed the difference. He smiled back at me and pointed to two of the biggest goblets I'd ever seen. "Gusher Sundae. You'll love it. You'll probably start making them at Bella Vista. Come on, Miss Alice Blue Gown, dig in."

There were five flavors of ice cream with three kinds of fruit and three kinds of syrup, bananas on the bottom, peanut butter in a hidden secret place and blobs of whipped cream topped with a cherry. Delicious. I think I could have eaten another one.

The bus ride home was like a trip in a fairy godmother's coach. We laughed over the movie. We laughed that I didn't spill my water in the ice cream shop. We laughed because, suddenly, we weren't enemies any more.

"I slid into the delicate little ice cream parlor chair and reached down to pull up my crazy hose."

Joe held my hand as we walked home from the bus stop. He put his arm almost around me and helped me up the steep stairs at their house. When he started to unlock the door, I wondered if he might kiss me. But Mrs. M turned on the porch light and opened the door from the other side. Not however, before he had put his big hand on my cheek and said, "Connee, you're sweet."

It was much later when Sally swept into the bedroom. I wasn't asleep. I was still playing over that delicious scene when Joe looked into my eyes. Sally flipped on the light and her eyes were dancing. "Guess what? Richard and I were named King and Queen of the dance. She whirled around making her full skirt go out in a circle. Her hair had grown longer and wavier than last summer. It fanned out over her shoulders. The sparkly necklace and earrings and her perfect complexion and deep brown eyes made her look like a princess. Well—a Queen. I got up and hugged her and she showed me the perfume he had given her as a gift. "I'm going to sleep with it under my pillow," she said in a dreamy voice and whirled again in front of the mirror.

She thought the hose episode was hilarious and wanted me to tell it again and again. I never did get to the part about coming home. I just told her the evening turned out to be perfect.

Long after she was asleep I lay thinking about how afraid I'd been to go to the dance. It had been my pride. Pride again, Grandmother. I walked softly over to my suitcase and took out my diary and pencil. *Dear, dear diary. I'm mixed up about pride.* Instead of writing more, I began thinking about that day with the paper dolls and how my pride had been hurt when I thought I'd given the wrong kind of gift and how it felt to realize I had danced without lessons. I remembered the way I'd let myself feel different and left out at the pool, even though Daddy had taught me that everyone is equal. But then, there was the good feeling about being friends with Sally, hard work and Bella Vista and helping Daddy at the store every day since he had his heart attack. I started writing again. *It's sure hard to know when it's good pride or bad pride, isn't it, dear God?*

All of a sudden I was filled with warm feelings. I thought of Mrs. M and Mr. Matofsky and Joe and all they'd done for me and I loved them. Hilda, too. And oh, how I loved Mother and Daddy and W. T. and Grandmother. And Lady and Jiggs and Kitty Thirteen and Frisky and my friends in Bentonville and Alice Hobbs and Julia Ann Paisley. Most of all, I loved SALLY.

I threw my covers back and stood up on the bed. I LOVE LIFE, I sang out and then—I began tap-dancing. I pushed back the throw rugs and I tapped up and down the room singing: *You—must have been a beautiful baby, you must have been a wonderful child. When you were only startin' to go to Kindergarten, I bet you drove the little boys wild....* Sally woke up and watched. "Are you crazy? Mom'll kill you. What about your ankle?"

Shaking my head and smiling—I went ahead singing and tapping. *And when it came to winnin' blue ribbons, I'll bet you showed the other girls how....*

A voice joined me loud and clear. Sally was up dancing with me! We tapped and sang in full voice: *I can see the judges' eyes as he handed you the prize...I bet you made the cutest bow.... OHHH, you must have been a beautiful baaaay-beeee 'cause baby...LOOK AT YOU NOW!!!!*

"Sally? Connee? Girls! What in the world is going on in there? Get to bed!"

"Yes Ma'm," we answered in unison diving for the same bed and pulling the covers over our heads.

"Friends?" we said together.

"Always."

Epilogue

Whitey May lived seven more years. He built May's Grocery and Filling Station into a thriving business, paid off his loan and saved enough for Gladys and W. T. (who became a pharmacist) to buy a drug store in Texas. Mr. and Mrs. Matofsky continued to come to their cottage in Bella Vista for many years and remained good friends with the Mays. The Linebargers lived until they were quite old. Their son, C.A. Linebarger, Jr., married Florence Ivy. They had three daughters named Carole A., C. Ann and Charity A., so that they all had the initials of C. A.

Connee's beloved Sally married an orchestra boy, named Jim Milan, who became a business executive with an oil company. They had a daughter, Leslie Anne, and a son, Jimmy. Sally died of cancer when she was only 41. Connee silently promised her to write this book so that Sally's grandchildren could hear the tales of their childhood. Connee was married to Ferris Norton, a minister for thirty years. They had four sons, Wendel, Wesley, Andrew and Timothy before Ferris died at age 52. Later, she married Don Waddell, a missionary, and "inherited" three more children: Betsy, Rebecca and Paul. Together they had many grandchildren and great grandchildren. Connee told all of them her stories of her wonderful childhood with Sally.

Joe and Connee dated a few times after they were grown. When he later changed his name to Martin for business reasons, they lost track of each other for many years. Connee's husband, Don, brought Connee (now Constance) back to her dear Bella Vista when they retired. She wrote news articles in "The Vista" about "old Bella Vista." One day she had a phone call from a Wanda Martin. She and her husband, Joe, were living in Bella Vista. He had just read one of the articles and wondered if she could be his Connee May? She was. Connee wanted to see him but Wanda felt she should wait a few days to see Joe since he was seriously ill. Joe died before she could see him again. She did, however, get to meet his wife and his son, Scott.

About the Author

Constance May Waddell returned to her childhood home in Bella Vista, Arkansas to fulfill a promise to write *Sally and Me*. She is a columnist for two Arkansas newspapers and has published feature articles in Dallas and Houston publications. Waddell is a retreat leader, speaker and vocalist.

As Ms. Senior Arkansas, 1995, she placed in the top ten in the Ms. Senior America contest. She is a swimmer and holds the state record for the 50M breaststroke in her age group in the Senior Olympics. She won two ribbons in the 2001 National Senior Olympics.

Waddell served as program director for an eight state retreat center and as a volunteer in mission work in the early 90's in Chile for the United Methodist Church.

Revisiting my rock.

She is an alumnus of Hendrix College and has a B.A. in Psychology from the U. of Missouri. She is a counselor in Bi-Polar Personal Growth and an instructor in Effectiveness Training for Women. While living in Dallas, she served as lay minister to women and children. Currently, Waddell is very involved in coordinating ministries and education for the Hispanic community in Northwest Arkansas.

About the Artist

Wendel Norton paints and sculpts at Hideout Mountain Studio in Snowball, Arkansas. He and his family built the studio from native timber high in the Ozark Mountains overlooking the Buffalo National River.

Norton has exhibited his work extensively, featuring shows in Little Rock, Dallas and New York City. He has illustrated collections of children's songs written by Paul Stookey (of Peter, Paul and Mary) and Jim Newton.

Norton is a graduate of Hendrix College in Conway, Arkansas. As a life member of The Art Students League in New York City, he studied sculpture with Philip Pavia. In St. Louis, he studied painting with Olive Chaffee.

Norton and his wife, Elizabeth, are partners in *Norton Arts*. Their company specializes in the conservation of fine and historic works of art. Projects have included Norman Rockwell's first known illustration of merit.

Artist Vanessa Norton assisted in the development of the collection of illustrations for this book.

Printed in the United States
4088

9 780759 679948